Praise for

START. RIGHT. NOW.

"Few books on education leadership are as mindful of their intended audience as this one is. Clear, convincing, and ceaselessly practical, *Start. Right. Now.* is soon to be a favored text in schools of education leadership. The collective brain trust among Whitaker, Zoul, and Casas is a national treasure to be referenced for years to come. Deeply professional and far from indifferent, the authors provide insight and principles for teachers and their leaders to confront professional hypocrisy, demonstrate deep knowledge in their daily practice, analyze and reflect on the effectiveness of actions, then revise practices based on those reflections. Tightly written, research infused, and including the voices of many of my favorite rising heroes in education, the book answers the hard questions of education leadership, including how to lead both formally and informally, the dynamic, fluid nature of excellence, the synergy between teaching and leading, responding to the 'no time' issue, planning for the future while attending to the present, and answering the plea, 'show me what it looks like,' definitively. The content is so inspiring, in fact, we have no choice but to drop the book and take action in our own schools."

—**Rick Wormeli**, author of *Fair Isn't Always Equal*,
columnist, and educator

"*Start. Right. Now.* gives the reader actionable ideas to implement that can make an immediate difference from any position. The experience of these educators, and the many whose stories they share in this book, makes this powerful and easy read a book that will help you make an immediate, positive impact on the culture of your classroom or school."

—**George Couros**, Innovative Teaching, Learning, and
Leadership Consultant, and author of *The Innovator's Mindset*

"Have you ever wanted to accomplish something but felt overwhelmed by the task? You try to focus, but all the components flood in? In *Start. Right. Now.*, you are taken on a journey that makes the process of moving forward not only doable, but creates an aha moment that lets you know movement is necessary. We can choose to stay stagnant, or we can choose to make things happen. Todd, Jimmy, and Jeff have created a powerful and entertaining book that will encourage you to dive into becoming exceptional!"

—LaVonna Roth, Creator and Founder of
Ignite Your SH.I.N.E.®

"As the Director of Innovation for Future Ready Schools, I've worked closely with over 750 school districts and 3,000 school administrators across the nation over the past few years. I have witnessed first-hand how these leaders are searching tirelessly to find innovative ways to create schools that better prepare students for their future. At a time when districts are rushing to fill their classrooms with the latest technology, leaders must first realize that leadership and school culture are the foundation to developing schools that are future ready. In *Start. Right. Now.*, Whitaker, Zoul, and Casas do an absolutely brilliant job laying out a framework to unlock the talent in every educator—both administrators and teachers. From vision and leadership, to creating a dynamic, relationship-empowered school culture with authentic learning experiences for all, this book absolutely nails it and equips both teachers and school leaders to consistently, intentionally, and actively know the way, show the way, go the way, and grow each day! If you're an educator working to shift instructional pedagogy in your classroom, or a school administrator leading the way, you will find this book to be one of your very best resources in your journey forward."

—Thomas C. Murray, Director of Innovation,
Future Ready Schools

"As both a third-grade classroom teacher and a teacher leader who is constantly striving to grow and improve for the kids and teachers I serve, I cannot give this book high enough praise. Todd, Jimmy, and Jeff list actionable and practical methods in which schools and educators can strive for success by delving into four core behaviors of excellence. Whether you are an educator of pre-K or a college professor, I can promise you will take away ideas from this book to empower you on your mission to achieve excellence."

—KAYLA DELZER, Elementary Educator,
TEDx and international keynote speaker

"The game has been changed! More than a book, *Start. Right. Now.* feels like a super-charged conversation with inspiring educators from all walks of life. It's a dialogue about the power of 'us.' Whitaker, Zoul, and Casas have amassed a huge supporting cast, and, as you read, you will feel them gripping your heart and empowering you to extend your reach and impact for kids."

—DR. BRAD GUSTAFSON, National Distinguished Principal and
author of *Renegade Leadership*

"If ever there was a time when teacher leadership was necessary for the excellence of education, it is now. This is an essential text that I wish I had the opportunity to read when I first began my own education career. Valuable and empowering, this book is a must-read for all educators. It is sure to have a profound impact on your professional practice."

—LAURA FLEMING, Librarian and author of *Worlds of Making:
Best Practices for Establishing a Makerspace for your School*

"Whitaker, Zoul, and Casas push the education conversation forward in their latest book. Educators who are serious about enhancing their professional growth and impacting the success of students must get their hands on a copy of this book today."

—BRAD CURRIE, #Satchat co-Founder and 2017 NJPSA
Visionary Assistant Principal of the Year

"Change isn't coming; it is already on our doorstep. The authors provide a compelling narrative on the specific actions all educators can make now in order to initiate sustainable change."

—ERIC SHENINGER, Senior Fellow, International Center for Leadership in Education

"Whitaker, Zoul, and Casas have written a remarkable book intended for anyone in education willing to take risks. With dozens of educators featured illustrating the pillars of *Start. Right. Now.*, the authors walk the talk in their belief that our students will benefit from people, not programs. I highly recommend this book for any teacher or school administrator who is striving to become future focused while attending to the present."

—MATT TOWNSLEY, Director of Instruction and Technology, Solon Community School District, Solon, Iowa

"Whitaker, Zoul, and Casas have accomplished a rare feat in academic writing. *Start. Right. Now.* is as informative as it is inspiring. For teachers who wish to lead and leaders who wish to teach, this is an essential read. Seriously. Pick it up, flip to page one, and enjoy the journey. Start. Right. Now."

—WESTON KIESCHNICK, Senior Fellow, International Center for Leadership in Education

"Todd Whitaker, Jeff Zoul, and Jimmy Casas did it again with their new book *Start. Right. Now.* Mindfully sharing their vision of leadership, they share the message of what they and great educators understand about knowing the way, showing the way, going the way, and growing each day. Breaking down each standard discussed and providing specific research and experience, not only of their own, but from educators in the field, the authors authentically provide a framework for change. Filled with inspiring words and commonsense approaches to bringing change to leadership, *Start. Right. Now.* will inspire you to do just that."

—STARR SACKSTEIN, Nationally Board Certified Teacher, teacher coach, and author

"This book resonated with me on many levels. As an experienced leader, it validated my leadership beliefs and values, and it challenged me to continue to grow and push the status quo. The personal vignettes and the 'Learn 4' tools at the end of each chapter give the reader guidance about how to live out each leadership standard. This book belongs in every school leader's toolbox!"

—**SANEE BELL**, Ed.D., Principal,
Morton Ranch Junior High, Katy, Texas

"Whitaker, Zoul, and Casas nailed it! Their book reads like an adventure story of lessons learned from themselves as well as other educational leaders around the United States! They share leadership insights to reaching a deeper level and weave in research-based practices and solid, practical strategies for teachers and leaders at all levels.

—**NEIL GUPTA**, Ed.D., Director of Secondary Education for
Worthington City Schools

"Todd, Jeff, and Jimmy have done it again. Their new book is encouraging, practical, and full of stories that cause the reader to move from 'Should I?' to 'How will I?' Educators at all levels and positions will benefit from their sound advice and uplifting words. It's definitely a must-read!"

—**JENNIFER HOGAN**, Ed.S. Assistant Principal of Curriculum
and Technology, Hoover High School

"Teachers are leaders and leaders are teachers. Whitaker, Zoul, and Casas embrace this mantra, as they outline a path toward excellence for all school personnel by defining critical leadership behaviors necessary for continual growth. Readers are provided with practical strategies certain to build leadership capacity within a variety of settings. *Start. Right. Now.* is a must for all professionals interested in getting better."

—**DAN BUTLER**, Principal, Epworth Elementary School,
Western Dubuque School District

"Whitaker, Casas, and Zoul offer a rare view of a practical approach to a different style of leadership that any educator can benefit from—whether you are a classroom teacher, an instructional specialist, or administrator. Each chapter includes successful practitioners who are exemplifying the strategy being presented. As an administrator, I love that these ideas are explained and modeled. They give me examples of people doing what I do—making it happen! Effective practices begin by identifying and answering the right questions when it comes to leadership, and this book is a great balance of sound information and proven practical, strategies to help any educator make a difference in the lives of students. *Start. Right. Now.* helps the reader develop a personal plan for action. It takes you from what you could do to what you can do. I highly recommend it!"

—**AMBER TEAMANN**, Principal, Whitt Elementary, Wylie, Texas

"Teachers, take heart. *Start. Right. Now.: Teach and Lead for Excellence* by Todd Whitaker, Jeffrey Zoul, and Jimmy Casas speaks directly to the leader in you! It starts strong with 'Teaching is Leading; Leading is Teaching.' This is the book teachers, coaches, and principals will use to launch needed professional-learning discussions around teaching and collaborative leadership. *Start. Right. Now.* delivers on readability and immediate application for all educators thanks to engaging and relevant stories. I absolutely recommend this book!"

—**LAURA GILCHRIST**, High School Teaching and
Learning Coach

"This is a book for teachers and administrators alike as it details the steps and high leverage actions necessary to achieve and sustain excellence over time. Sprinkled with first-person accounts from the nation's top educators, the book combines the authors' extensive expertise with elements of leadership that are a must for any staff."

—**TREVOR GREENE**, NASSP National Principal of the Year

"The emphasis in this book on the alignment between professed beliefs and enacted behaviors is critically important. If we want significant changes in learning and teaching to occur, we have to stop paying lip service to school transformation and actually start implementing the instructional and organizational practices that make it happen. The status quo of traditional schooling won't go down without a fight and our own entrenched mindsets and practices impede the progress that we say we want. This new book, which includes profiles of model educators, practitioner reflection questions, and numerous, concrete examples of school dilemmas and successes, will help teachers and administrators reflect upon what they are doing (and not doing) so that they can 'walk the walk' when it comes to their own local change efforts."

—DR. SCOTT MCLEOD, Associate Professor of Educational Leadership; Founding Director of CASTLE; University of Colorado Denver

START.
RIGHT.
NOW.

Teach and Lead for Excellence

TODD WHITAKER, JEFFREY ZOUL, JIMMY CASAS

Start. Right. Now.
© 2017 by Todd Whitaker, Jeffrey Zoul, Jimmy Casas

This book is available at special discounts when purchased in quantity for use as premiums, promotions, fundraisers, or for educational use. For inquiries and details, contact the publisher at shelley@daveburgessconsulting.com.

Published by Dave Burgess Consulting, Inc.
San Diego, CA
http://daveburgessconsulting.com

Cover Design by Genesis Kohler
Editing and Interior Design by My Writers' Connection

Library of Congress Control Number: 2016961171
Paperback ISBN: 978-0-9969896-8-8
Ebook ISBN: 978-0-9969896-9-5
First Printing: January 2017

DEDICATION

Todd would like to dedicate this book to his mother, Avis Whitaker, who always seems to *Know the Way* to excellence...

Jeff would like to dedicate this book to his mother, Jerri Zoul, for consistently *Showing the Way* to excellence...

Jimmy would like to dedicate this book to his mom and dad, Paul and Gloria Casas, who have helped him understand the importance of *Going the Way*. Thank you, Mom and Dad, for always modeling the importance of relationships, serving others, building community, a strong work ethic, and never settling for good, but aspiring for excellence...

Finally, Todd, Jeff, and Jimmy wish to dedicate this book to every member of their personal and professional learning networks for consistently helping them *Grow Each Day*.

CONTENTS

TEACHING IS LEADING;
LEADING IS TEACHING

Effective leaders are, first and foremost, good teachers. We are in the education business.
–John Wooden

Great leaders, as Coach Wooden noted, are indeed great teachers. Conversely, great teachers are also great leaders. In fact, let's look at the quote again, transposing the words, "leaders" and "teachers": *Effective teachers are, first and foremost, good leaders.* Our very best leaders know that they must teach those they lead, and our very best teachers realize they are leaders and behave accordingly.

We have visited thousands of schools around the world during the past several decades, and wherever we go, we notice this reality playing out before our eyes. We observe great teachers exhibiting amazing leadership skills, not only in their classrooms, but also throughout their schools, districts, communities, and beyond. We also observe educators in "official" leadership roles, such as principals and superintendents, taking an active role in teaching those with whom they serve. They simultaneously teach specific content and skills and lead by example as they seek to continually grow and improve themselves, their colleagues, and their organizations.

We are avid collectors of quotes about leaders and leadership, and teachers and teaching. In perusing our favorite quotes about leaders and leadership, we realized an interesting phenomenon: In virtually every instance, if we replace the word "leader" with "teacher," or "leadership" with "teaching," the quotation loses nothing in translation. In fact, the meaning remains just as strong. In addition to the Wooden quote, we've listed a few more examples below to make this case. These quotations make a point about great leaders and great leadership, and each applies equally well to great teachers and great teaching. Try replacing the words "leader" or "leadership" with "teacher" or "teaching" in each:

> **"As a leader [teacher], your principal job is to create an operating environment where others can do great things."**
> —Richard Teerlink

> **"No person can be a great leader [teacher] unless he takes genuine joy in the successes of those under him."**
> —W. A. Nance

> **"A good leader [teacher] inspires others with confidence in him; a great leader [teacher] inspires them with confidence in themselves."** —Unknown

> **"Leadership [Teaching] is practiced not so much in words as in attitude and in actions."** —Harold S. Geneen

> **"Leadership [Teaching] and learning are indispensable to each other."** —John F. Kennedy

These quotations—along with many others we have collected—validate our belief that much of what makes a great leader is also what makes a great teacher, and vice versa. We have come to believe that these two terms have much more in common than some might think and, in fact, are interchangeable in our very best classrooms and schools. Specifically, we have noticed that in the very best schools we have visited, the lines between "teacher" and "leader" tend to blur, with classroom teachers taking on active leadership roles and building principals devoting time to directly teaching students and staff. We began to wonder exactly what behaviors these excellent teachers and excellent leaders both exhibited in their daily lives as educators. What was it that made them stand out as truly exceptional? Our discoveries, based on our many years of observing such educators, are the focus of this book.

FROM BELIEFS TO BEHAVIORS

In nearly all the schools in which we have worked, the vast majority of educators share many similar beliefs, at least in a big-picture sense. Visit any school around the world, and presumably all educators working there would tell you that they believe all kids can learn, that we should try to foster lifelong learning within our students, and that we should engage our kids in the 4 C's of twenty-first-century learning: Communication, Collaboration, Creativity, and Critical Thinking. We have also noticed, however, that merely professing to believe in these things is not enough. Truly exceptional teachers and leaders move beyond beliefs, exhibiting specific, observable, and intentional behaviors that turn these beliefs into reality. Although amazing educators share many similar beliefs, they also have strong, *differing* beliefs about education and their roles in our noble profession and are often quite vocal about sharing them. Regardless of whether their beliefs mirror those of their colleagues, the educators we consider to be excellent are quick to align their beliefs with their actions.

On the other hand, each of us has worked with educators who, when asked, would say they share the exact same beliefs as those expressed by their truly exceptional colleagues, yet exhibit behaviors that simply do not align with these beliefs. They "believe" all kids can learn, but they begin the school year assuming a certain percentage of students will fail their course. They "believe" in collaborative school cultures, but issue top-down mandates. They "believe" in student-centered classrooms, but spend a majority of class time lecturing and assigning worksheets. Or they "believe" that principals should be highly visible, yet find they are too busy to get in classrooms themselves each day. A key difference between our mediocre teachers and leaders and our truly exceptional ones is the fact that truly exceptional teachers and leaders walk the talk, exhibiting behaviors that are consistent with their beliefs.

When interviewing teaching or principal candidates, we sometimes ask, "Do you consider yourself more a 'doer' or a 'dreamer?'" Often the answers are revealing, but, truthfully, we hope to find the perfect blend of these two apparent extremes within the professional makeup of those with whom we serve. Truly excellent teachers and school administrators realize the need for both "dreaming" and "doing." They consider their beliefs their "dreams," and their behaviors are what they will "do" to make these dreams come true.

VALUES IN ACTION? MISSION ACCOMPLISHED!

Virtually every school we visit has a mission statement. However, only a small minority of these schools have actually managed to make the mission statement the driving force of the decisions made and the actions taken by staff members. In most schools, the statement is merely a nice collection of words on a wall that has no impact whatsoever on student or staff performance, outcomes, or satisfaction. The variable is not the mission statement itself (since almost all schools have one), but the actions and decisions that team members make because of the mission statement.

We believe in the power of mission statements that are created with intention and communicated and acted upon regularly. Despite the hit-or-miss nature of mission statement efficacy that we have observed at schools around the world, we remain advocates for investing in this process as a starting point for excellence. Simon Sinek, author of *Start with Why*, makes a compelling case for the importance of starting any worthy venture by asking, "Why?" We view the school or district mission statement as the ultimate answer to that organization's "Why?" Moreover, we suspect that many outstanding teachers and administrators also start by examining why they do what they do, going so far as to adopt a personal mission statement by which they live on a daily basis. Some may actually have written out those statements. Others may not have a mission statement actually written out and posted anywhere in their classroom or office, but we suspect that if one were to observe them in action over a period of time, it would not take long before we could discern their "mission" by the behaviors they consistently exhibit.

The organizational mission statement should succinctly answer the questions, "Why do we (as a classroom, school, or district) exist? What is our core purpose for being?" Our purpose in this book is not to answer these questions; instead, we simply wish to suggest that examining our true purpose—as individual educators and as teams of educators working together—is a worthwhile and often revealing activity.

Ask: Why do we (as a classroom, school, or district) exist?

Even with a compelling mission statement in place—one that is known by all members of the organization, communicated regularly among many in the organization, and used frequently as a driving force for decision making—having an overarching description of why we exist is still not as important as the consistent behaviors each team member exhibits as they go about their jobs. Successful school leaders know this, and so, shortly after agreeing to adopt a mission statement, they also identify the values by which the members of their organization will operate to ensure that the school stays mission-focused. We equate values with behaviors, or commonly held commitments that team members make regarding non-negotiable actions to which they will adhere over time.

For example, we often see school mission statements promoting the belief that "all kids can learn." Sounds noble, but again, what actions will educators within such schools take when some students do not learn, at least not in the way we assumed they would, or within the allotted time for which we have planned? Commonly held values—created collaboratively and agreed to collectively—can help to answer such questions. By themselves, such value statements documented in words are no more effectual than meaningless mission statements. However, when these values statements are backed up with specific actions or behaviors that team members live out and hold each other accountable for, amazing things can happen. Values in action result in missions accomplished!

THE 4 CORE BEHAVIORS OF EXCELLENCE

The importance of commonly held core values, which play out as actions taken on a daily basis to ensure that the mission is accomplished, cannot be overstated. In addition, we have observed that in high-performing schools staffed by high-performing teachers and leaders and filled with energized, engaged, and connected students, there is also a shared vision of excellence. Teachers are not there merely to deliver lessons, principals do not exist simply to react to situations that arise, and students are not passive receivers of instruction. Instead, each member of these educational communities actively pursues their own learning and leadership opportunities. In such schools, standards of excellence are clearly in place for students and staff. These expectations for excellence are carefully established at the outset. They are reiterated not only every school year, but also each day, to consistently remind everyone in the school what the work is, why it matters, and how to go about accomplishing it. There are likely hundreds, if not thousands, of specific daily actions taking place in such schools that work together to make these high-performing schools stand out from others. Those activities can be classified into four overarching areas, three of which are often attributed to leadership guru John Maxwell, who defines a leader as one who, "knows the way, goes the way, and shows the way." To this definition (which we apply to teachers as well as administrators), we would add the critical component of intentional, personal, *daily* growth: *A leader is one who knows the way, shows the way, goes the way, and grows each day.* We will expand on these four elements of excellence in the subsequent chapters of this book. For now, here is a brief summary of the four core behaviors that distinguish the very best from all the rest.

To start, great teachers and great leaders **know the way.** Whether they are teaching a lesson on astronomy, working with colleagues on a new intervention strategy, developing a social/emotional learning curriculum, or helping a student shoot a basketball, these educators know their stuff. Not every leader or teacher knows the most about every aspect of their job, but when they are leading others—whether students or staff—they take the time to make sure they have learned as much as possible prior to enlisting others to follow their lead.

A leader is one who knows the way, shows the way, goes the way, and grows each day.

Great teachers and leaders also **show the way.** One of the best pieces of advice about writing fiction that we have heard is the adage that the writer must "show" rather than "tell" what is happening. We recall a talk given by Robert Newton Peck, author of many young adult novels, including *A Day No Pigs Would Die*, driving this point home to a group of student authors by imploring, "Don't just say the fat lady screamed; bring her on and let her scream!" Great teachers and leaders know the importance of showing, rather than merely telling. They may start by explaining how something is done or why an action needs to be taken, but they move beyond mere telling to showing how it can or will be done and painting the picture of precisely why the work needs doing.

In addition to knowing the way and showing the way, great teachers and leaders **go the way.** They teach and lead by modeling, living out what they expect others to do by doing it themselves. When teachers model lifelong learning for their students by connecting with educators around the world to find new resources, enroll in a graduate program for an advanced degree, or research new ways to teach a math concept, they go the way that they also want their students to go. When administrators make positive calls home to parents or write positive notes to staff members for a job well done, they, too, are going the way they want others to go.

Finally, great teachers and leaders **grow each day.** They not only grow themselves, but also grow those around them. They are professionals who are always striving to get better, never allowing the fact that they are good at what they do to get in the way of wanting to be great at what they do. They carve out time in each busy day to learn something new, practice a skill they already have, or find a way to help someone else reach a goal. They not only "believe" in a growth mindset, but exhibit such a mindset by actively seeking out and acquiring new knowledge and skills for themselves and others.

The variable that distinguishes truly great schools from merely good schools is, of course, the people working within the schools. The importance of school facilities, technology, literacy programs, and demographic populations pale in comparison to the quality of the school's teachers and administrators. Simply put, if you have a school staffed with great teachers and administrators, well, you have a great school! We believe that teachers and leaders become truly exceptional when they consistently, intentionally, and actively *know the way, show the way, go the way, and grow each day.*

TEACHERS WHO LEAD

Some of the greatest teachers are also some of the greatest leaders. But what do we mean when we talk about "teacher leadership," and is that different from a classroom teacher who is also a great leader? The topic of teacher leadership is one much written about and discussed in recent years, and in May 2011, the Teacher-Leader Model Standards were released in Washington, D.C.[1] Educational researchers define teacher leadership as "the process by which teachers, individually or collectively, influence their colleagues, principals, and other members of the school community to improve teaching and learning practices with the aim of increased student learning and achievement."[2] Although we understand and respect this definition, we find it limiting in the sense that it suggests teachers labeled as leaders influence "colleagues, principals, and other members of the school community." We maintain this list leaves out two equally—if not more—important stakeholders: students and the teacher leader herself.

Harrison and Killion define a teacher leader this way:

A teacher who assumes formally or informally one or more of a wide array of leadership roles to support school and student success. Examples include [roles such as] instructional specialist, curriculum specialist, classroom supporter, learning facilitator, mentor, school leader (e.g., serving on a school committee, acting as a grade-level or department chair, supporting school initiatives, or representing the school on community or district task forces or committees), data coach, catalyst for change, resource provider, or learner.[3]

Although this definition does include the concept of teacher as learner and suggests such leadership roles can be either formal or informal, it still strikes us as describing a teacher who only leads when not in the actual position of teaching students. It is certainly true that some amazing teachers leave the classroom and become equally amazing leaders in full-time roles such as instructional coaches, curriculum specialists, or even school administrators. It is also logical to suggest that some amazing teachers who remain in the classroom full time take on additional leadership roles outside of their regular classroom duties, whether they are serving as a mentor to colleagues or as a department/grade-level chair. We do not wish to minimize the importance or validity of either of these "teacher-as-leader" scenarios. But we do want to emphasize the importance of the leadership demonstrated each and every day in classrooms by outstanding teachers who teach and lead their students on wide-ranging journeys—journeys relating to their content area as well as life itself.

In this book, when we refer to "teachers who lead" or "teacher leaders" or "teacher leadership" we are referring to current classroom teachers who are experts at teaching their students and experts at leading their students, as well as others in their school communities. Teachers who lead see themselves, first and foremost, as classroom teachers charged with teaching and leading the students they serve. Although many teachers who lead likely recognize (if only in private moments of self-reflection) that their students and peers consider them leaders, we have worked with a number of teachers we consider to be excellent leaders who are surprised when we point out their unique talent for leading others. These humble teachers seem to think of leadership as an esoteric field of study reserved for a select few. They may think leadership is beyond their sphere of influence and believe that leadership entails bigger, more profound actions than the ones they take on a daily basis as they go about their job teaching students. Nothing could be further from the truth, in our opinion. Virtually no job opens itself up to the possibility of influencing others more than that of a classroom teacher. And no acts of leadership are larger than the actions teachers take each day to lead their students on a path to future success. In fact, we find that it is often the simplest acts that educators perform—with intention and on a consistent basis—that have the greatest influence and impact on others.

What is it, then, about truly exemplary teachers that separates them from others in terms of how they are viewed as both teachers and leaders?

Teachers who lead know the way. They know their stuff. They know the content they teach inside and out. More importantly, they know their students inside and out—what they are good at, what they need to get better at, and what their interests are. They know what is most important, what they can filter out, and why it matters. They also know how to respond when they do not know something, typically by saying something along the lines of, "I don't know; let's find out."

Teachers who lead also show the way. They show others how to get better, whether that means helping them to acquire a new skill or taking an existing skill to the next level. Whether working with students or colleagues, they do not settle for simply explaining how to do something; instead, they demonstrate—often in a variety of ways—how to do something.

Teachers who lead also go the way. They are master "modelers" who act in ways they want others to act. They have extremely high expectations for others and even higher expectations for themselves. They often take time to establish such expectations for their students at length on the first day of class—and then spend the remaining days of the school year building relationships with students so that their students will want to meet these expectations. Teachers who lead walk the talk and are not afraid to do themselves what they are asking of others.

Finally, *teachers who lead grow each day.* They never rest on their laurels and never think "good enough" is good enough. They are constantly striving to become better at what they do. Moreover, they push their students to get better and better at what they do, knowing that the standards they are required to teach are the floor for all students, but the ceiling for none. They motivate themselves by connecting with other outstanding teachers in their school, district, and around the world. Teachers who lead possess a growth mindset for themselves and encourage their students to adopt a growth mindset, as well.

Teachers lead by doing and, more importantly, by being. Teachers who lead come in all shapes and sizes. Some are veteran teachers who have been teaching and leading with excellence for many, many years. Others are first-year teachers whose performance immediately stands out. Some teach in urban schools, others serve in rural communities. Some are male; others are female. Some teach one subject all day long at the high-school level while still others teach a variety of subjects to elementary school students each day. Some of these excellent teachers who lead are extroverted, gregarious human beings, while others are more reserved. Although these excellent teachers who lead are different in many ways, they have at least four critical attributes in common that contribute to their success: *they know the way, show the way, go the way, and grow each day.*

LEADERS WHO TEACH

Some of the greatest leaders are also great teachers. In the field of education, this means that building and district administrators do not stop teaching when they move from the classroom into formal leadership roles. The principal as "instructional leader" or "lead learner" are concepts much in vogue in recent years to the point that many principals with whom we have worked actually use the title "lead learner" in lieu of the more traditional title of "principal." Of course, simply calling oneself the "lead learner" has little impact on the role of the school leader or on the success of students and teachers in those schools. Actually behaving as the school's lead learner, however, can make a difference in the school's culture and, ultimately, in the performance of its students and teachers. School and district leaders we have known and observed who truly embody the lead-learner mentality and model lifelong learning are not merely learning for the sake of their own growth; they are continually learning and growing so that they, in turn, can teach others what they are learning. Learning leaders seek learning opportunities for a variety of reasons, one of which is their desire to serve as *leaders who teach.*

Leaders who teach view themselves not as the school's or district's "lead knower," but they do consider themselves lead learners, who then share their learning with staff, students, parents, community members, and the world beyond their school community. Roland Barth, author of *Improving Schools from Within*, maintains that if students are to grow and learn, their teachers must grow and learn, too. We maintain that if teachers are to grow and learn, principals also must continually grow and learn. In fact, the title *principal* emanates from the concept of the person in such a role serving as the *principal teacher*. Although school and district administrators are charged with scads of duties and responsibilities, many of which are operational or managerial in nature, the very best leaders never forget that the core business of their schools is learning. They realize that their core focus must, therefore, be on learning, including the learning not only of students in their schools, but also adults—starting with themselves.

The very best leaders never forget that the core business of their schools is learning.

School and district administrators who focus on learning know that it makes a difference. In a large-scale study of the impact of school principals on student achievement, Viviane Robinson and her colleagues found five leadership domains that had significant effect sizes (shown in parentheses) on student achievement:[4]

1. Establishing goals and expectations (0.42)

2. Resourcing strategically (0.31)

3. Ensuring quality teaching (0.42)

4. Leading teacher learning and development (0.84)

5. Ensuring an orderly and safe environment (0.27)

Although each of these five domains is impactful, the domain of "leading teacher learning and development," including participating as a learner alongside teachers, is twice as powerful as the next highest behavior. Knowing the influence their learning can have on teachers and students, excellent leaders act intentionally about the learning they undertake and the ways in which they share their learning. They also know what serving as a lead learner does not mean: it does not mean knowing the most about any single subject area. In fact, we hope that teachers in various content areas actually know their content far more deeply than any administrator. We have never worked in a school or district in which the principal or superintendent knew more about the math curriculum, the fine arts curriculum, social/emotional learning, or the Common Core State Standards than every other educator with whom they served. However, we have worked in schools and districts led by principals and superintendents who took an active interest in learning about each of these areas and, more importantly, actively sharing what they had learned with others while also empowering those with even more knowledge in each area to lead the way.

In this book, when we refer to "leaders who teach," "building leaders," or "educational leaders," we are referring to current school or district employees serving in official leadership capacities, including principals, assistant principals, superintendents, curriculum specialists, instructional coaches, department chairs, and other formal roles traditionally considered "non-teaching" roles. Of course, we make the case that these roles are anything but. In fact, we include, as a core component of their job description, the capacity and willingness to teach others. We focus on administrators and others who are experts at leading their departments, schools, and districts—and are passionate about continuing their own learning and sharing that learning with those they lead. Although many outstanding school and district leaders may not acknowledge it, they are looked to by teachers in their schools as teachers themselves—people who guide and influence their own teaching. We have worked with some leaders who we consider among the best teachers we know. To be honest, we have also worked with administrators who seem to have forgotten that learning is the primary business of a school. They have subordinated the importance of their own teaching and learning behaviors to less impactful managerial priorities. To be sure, the demands upon school leaders in various roles make it easy to lose sight, at times, of what is most important. They may simply think that actively teaching and learning as an administrator is beyond their realm of primary responsibility. Again, nothing could be further from the truth. The very best leaders manage to find ways to focus on teaching and learning themselves, while still accomplishing the many other tasks associated with their roles. Whether taking a few minutes at the start of every faculty or leadership team meeting to teach others what they have learned or engaging the entire staff or team in a book study, *leaders who teach* continue to find ways to grow, improve, and share their learning with those they lead.

So what separates truly exemplary leaders from others in terms of how they are viewed not only as leaders, but also as teachers? In short, it is the very same four behaviors that separate mediocre teachers from exemplary teachers. We hope you will pardon just a bit of redundancy here, but we feel it is important in making our case that the same four behaviors that make certain teachers stand out as excellent are identical to the four behaviors that distinguish excellent school leaders from mediocre ones.

Leaders who teach know the way. They know their stuff. Whether they are superintendents, principals, or department leaders, they know a great deal about all aspects of their job and stay current on new research relating to their duties and responsibilities. In the same way that the best history teachers are also students of history, school leaders are students of leadership, reading constantly, seeking out the advice of leaders they respect, visiting leaders in other schools and districts, and staying active through social media outlets to share what they are learning while also borrowing ideas from colleagues. Excellent leaders know what research reveals as best practices in terms of leadership. More importantly, they know the people they lead inside and out, what these people are good at, what they need to get better at, and what their interests are. They know what is most important, what they can filter out, and why it matters.

Leaders who teach also show the way. They show others how to get better, whether that means helping them to acquire a new skill or to take an existing skill to the next level. Whether working with students, teachers, or fellow administrators, they do not settle for simply explaining how to do something; instead, they *demonstrate*—often in a variety of ways—how to do something. These leaders build consensus around a common set of values for running the district, school, or department. They consistently share an exciting dream of the future and show those they lead how their long-term interests can be realized by enlisting in this common vision. They paint the big picture for the team, communicating top district and department priorities along with plans to improve results.

Leaders who teach also go the way. They are master modelers who act in ways they want others to act. They have extremely high expectations for others, and even higher expectations for themselves. Much like teachers, they often set such expectations for those they lead on the first day of a school year or on the first day of a school or district initiative—and then focus much of their subsequent efforts on building relationships with others so that the people they lead will actually want to meet these expectations. Leaders who teach are not afraid to do themselves what they are asking of others. They set the example for what they expect of others and follow through on the promises and commitments they make. They are consistently present, visible, and accessible throughout the school or district.

Finally, ***leaders who teach grow each day.*** Much like excellent teachers, they are constantly striving to become better at what they do as leaders. Moreover, they also push those they lead to get better and better at what they do. These leaders motivate themselves by connecting with other outstanding leaders in their schools, districts, and around the world. They seek out challenging opportunities that test their own skills and abilities and challenge others to try out new and innovative ways to do their work. Leaders who teach possess a growth mindset for themselves and encourage those they lead to adopt a growth mindset.

Leaders lead by doing and, more importantly, by being. Leaders who teach—just like teachers who lead—come in all shapes and sizes. Although these excellent leaders who teach are different in many ways, they have at least four critical attributes in common that contribute to their success: *they know the way, show the way, go the way, and grow each day.*

Who This Book Is for and How to Use It

This book is about what excellent teachers and leaders do that sets them apart. In this introduction, we started the conversation by suggesting that what sets apart truly excellent teachers and leaders from their peers are behaviors that, generally speaking, are the same whether they are teachers or administrators. We made the case that the very best teachers are leaders and the very best leaders are teachers. Throughout this book, we will be sharing our own stories as well as the stories of other educators we have come to know and respect. We will look at where these excellent teachers and leaders focus their attention, how they spend their time and energy, what guides their decisions, and, most importantly, how we can learn from them so we can grow and improve—as teachers and leaders.

We wrote this book for a wide audience of educators—educators at any grade level from Pre-K to higher education. We also wrote this book for educators serving in any role, from school principals, to high-school teachers, to university professors, to school superintendents, to librarians, to elementary- and middle-school teachers. Although excellent teachers and leaders vary widely in geographic locations, job titles, personal traits, and many other factors, what they have in common is also revealing: a zest for lifelong learning, a need to share what they know and learn from others, a desire to associate with other educators who are equally energized about our noble profession, and a willingness to change and take risks.

The format of this book is straightforward. We hope this introductory chapter provides context on the importance and power of exemplary teaching and leading. The following four chapters focus on a single standard of teaching and leading excellence that teachers and leaders intentionally set for themselves to perform at high levels, continually learn and grow, and improve the lives of those they serve and those with whom they serve. A concluding chapter attempts to connect these four behaviors into a composite picture of what it looks like to serve as an exemplary teacher and leader, and how we can use this information to transform our classrooms and schools into better places in which to teach and learn.

The bulk of this book consists of the four behaviors that the very best educators do differently. These four variables—*Know the Way,*

Show the Way, Go the Way, and *Grow Each Day*—are introduced at the outset of each chapter. We provide a list of indicators for each, a snapshot specifying what actions and behaviors great educators take to exemplify the overall standard of excellence. We then briefly summarize what it means to "do" the standard for excellence, why it matters, and how we have seen these behaviors play out in schools around the country. We will make a case for why doing each of these four things will not only make you better at what you do, but also how doing these things will change the way you look at education overall. We provide our own insights as well as examples from others. From an organizational standpoint, we close each of the four "Standards 4 Excellence" chapters with three short sections to tie it all together:

I. Teach 4—For each *Teaching and Leading for Excellence* standard, we list four educators who are currently serving primarily as classroom teachers from our personal and professional learning network (P²LN) who we believe stand as models in the particular area written about in that chapter. We share a short reflection from each of these four educators related to the main topic of the chapter.

II. Lead 4—For each *Teaching and Leading for Excellence* standard, we list four educators currently serving in a formal educational leadership role from our P²LN who we believe stand as models in the particular area written about in that chapter. We share a short reflection from each of these four educators related to the main topic of the chapter.

III. Learn 4—For each *Teaching and Leading for Excellence* standard, we share four resources / tools / action steps you can use to further develop yourself in that particular area. There are links to resources that we have learned about through our work in schools around the world or that we have used ourselves as teachers and leaders.

Thank you for joining us in our personal quest to continually grow and improve. One way we get better is by identifying what excellence looks like in action and sharing our findings with others. The next step is even more important: taking the step to *start*. No matter where you have been or what your classroom or school looks like at the moment, there is no better time to start your journey to excellence than right now. Don't wait. *Start. Right. Now.* Our hope is that you will find new ideas in this book to help you live out a life of teaching and leading with excellence.

KNOW THE WAY

*The best teachers are artists who know
the science of teaching.*
—Richard Bankert

Excellent teachers (and leaders) are both artists and scientists. They possess a thorough knowledge and understanding of the theory, research, and best practices related to the fields of pedagogy and leadership. At the same time, they have mastered the equally (if not more) important soft skills of their role, such as communicating, adapting, collaborating, responding, relationship building, and problem solving. They excel at the practice of empathy, and they seek to truly understand those with whom they work and what motivates them. They know that, before they can lead or teach others, they must first know themselves. They also know precisely what it is they are trying to teach or lead and why it is important for others to know this, too. Great teachers and leaders are scientists and artists who know the way to excellence.

DEFINING THE STANDARD: KNOWING THE WAY FOR EXCELLENCE

The first standard of teaching and leading excellence exhibited by innovative, passionate, and persistent educators with whom we have worked is all about knowledge: knowledge of themselves, their colleagues, students, best practices, future trends, and the overall mission of their organization, as well as their role in fulfilling this mission. Below, we've outlined this standard in some detail, including indicators to look for, but in short, here's what it means to **Know the Way:** **Possessing extensive and intimate knowledge about every aspect of the work and acting upon this knowledge to fulfill individual, team, and organizational missions.**

STANDARD OF EXCELLENCE #1
Excellent Teachers and Leaders Know the Way

Excellent teachers and leaders know the mission, vision, values, and goals of their districts, schools, departments, and classrooms. They possess deep knowledge of all aspects relating to education in general and their role specifically. They are keenly aware of their strengths and limitations. They actively seek to learn all they can about the students and staff with whom they serve.

INDICATORS

- Possesses knowledge of effective teaching and leadership practices, characteristics, and behaviors

- Possesses knowledge of core content relating to assigned areas of responsibility

- Demonstrates clarity about their teaching and/or leadership philosophy

- Is knowledgeable about all aspects of the district: its schools, the school community, its students, and its staff

- Understands the critical work of schools

- Possesses and demonstrates an extremely high level of self-knowledge; is well aware of their own strengths and weaknesses

- Is informed about current best practices relating to various educational domains, including curriculum, instruction, assessment, school leadership, and professional learning

- Exudes confidence, not arrogance, and instills such confidence in others

- Identifies top priorities and develops plans for improved results

- Continues to expand knowledge by asking questions and seeking input/feedback

- Speaks with genuine conviction and confidence about the purpose of the work and why it matters

- Finds ways to learn more about the students they serve and the colleagues with whom they work

- **Focuses on the question, "Why do we exist as a district, school, department, or classroom?" and behaves in ways aligned to fulfilling this mission**

Why It Matters

A cornerstone of success in any endeavor is possessing a deep understanding about all aspects of the challenge before us. A comment we often hear from educators describing fellow educators whom they hold in high regard is: "They really know their stuff!" As educators, we are charged with a host of responsibilities, but our core business can be pared down to a single word: learning.

Success in learning begins by acquiring vitally important knowledge and skills. By this, we do not mean traditional content-specific or intellectual knowledge, but the kind of knowledge that is available to each of us—if we deem it important enough to pursue. The essence of this first standard of excellence is knowing why we even exist as learning organizations and as individuals within such organizations. In our experience, the best educators make the time and expend the effort to acquire this knowledge, which includes self-knowledge, as well as deep knowledge about other staff, students, parents, and community members, in addition to educational history and future trends.

Truly outstanding educators begin their journey along the path of excellence by knowing their stuff.

Excellent educators, including those highlighted throughout this book, are lifelong learners, leaders, and doers who succeed because they actively and intentionally pursue—with laser-like focus—new knowledge aimed at improving themselves and those around them. They live in the moment, making the most of every second of every day, but they never forget the overarching purpose of why they do what they do. Their actions may, at times, seem random to a casual observer; however, almost nothing about what they do is random. Instead, their actions are executed with strategic intention and planning. Teachers and leaders who know the way are never cocky, but they are confident. Leaders who know the way realize that the greatest gift they can give their teachers is the gift of confidence. Teachers, in turn, realize that the greatest gift they can give their students is the gift of confidence. This confidence comes, primarily, from knowing what they are doing and why they are doing it. They have identified the current status of the situation, examined all possible next steps, and identified the most important area of focus for right now. Knowledge breeds confidence, and confidence breeds risk taking and opportunities for growth.

Truly outstanding educators begin their journey along the path of excellence by knowing their stuff. They realize that before they can show anyone else the path to success, they must first know it themselves. They also realize that such paths typically include a fair amount of twists, turns, obstacles, and detours; although they anticipate these and even embrace these as natural and inevitable happenings, they never take their eye off their ultimate purpose or destination. The work of an educator is noble and important work. It is also highly complex, demanding, stressful, and constantly evolving. Excellent teachers and leaders know this and, therefore, invest significant time to equip themselves with the knowledge needed to succeed.

What It Looks Like

Start with "Why?" then, "Where?"

Excellent teachers and leaders always keep in mind where they are going and, more importantly, why they are heading in that direction. They begin by focusing on the "Why?" of their very existence:

- Why do they serve in the roles they do?

- Why does the school even exist; what is its core purpose?

- Why did they decide to enter this noble profession?

- What is their "true north" that guides what they do?

This leadership behavior is akin to the concept of a mission statement and, not surprisingly, educators who stand out in this regard are often referred to, with respect, as being "on a mission" or "mission focused." Typically, this mission is laser-like and focused on the students, school, and district in which they serve. Mission-focused educators face the same level of stress, personal challenges, office politics, and frustrations common to all educators, but they rarely lose sight of their ultimate purpose for existing: to create a tomorrow that is better than today for their students by ensuring that each student continually grows and learns. To these teachers and leaders, engaging a student in an authentic learning experience or collaborating with a colleague on an innovative project takes precedence over adult-centered debates such as duty rosters or lunch schedules. Instead of focusing on what is best for the adults in the building, they constantly ask themselves, "How will this decision impact our students?"

Knowing the "why" of what they do and keeping their purpose in mind at all times is a consistent trait of excellent educators. Likewise, these teachers and leaders also continuously focus on the "where" of what it is they do. They intentionally focus on where they are currently, where they need to get to ultimately, and where they need to get to next in order to close the gap. They start with the end in mind and plan accordingly.

Like teachers and administrators everywhere, they never have enough time to do everything they need and want to do. Unlike some, however, one thing they do to maximize their time is eliminate complaining. By not complaining about the many frustrations they face—including, ironically, how little time they have—great educators actually save time that others waste. With the time they do have available to them (the same as we all have, incidentally), they adopt habits and create rituals designed to make the most of every precious minute.

Tony Schwartz, a well-known author and business consultant, talks about such "productivity rituals" as consciously created expressions of fierce intention. Excellent educators exhibit an almost "fierce" intention in knowing where they need to go next and how to get there.

They establish rituals and routines, and they follow these consistently to minimize both the possibility of wasting time and the occurrence of unexpected events. These educators do not happen upon such rituals and routines by chance; instead, they learn from experience how best to set up their schedules—and those with whom they work—for success. Great educators who consciously create and purposefully adhere to productivity rituals do so because of the passion they have for helping others succeed. They are determined to succeed, and they plan accordingly—even, as Schwartz suggests, "fiercely."

Educators who succeed in "knowing the way" to excellence know why they entered the education profession and why they continue to serve. They know that students are the ultimate "why" for schools. They also know where their current "Point A" is as individuals and as part of their organization. They then plan intentional next steps designed to move to "Point B" on the path leading to where they, their school, their teachers, and their students need to ultimately be in order to fulfill their mission.

Know Thyself

One variable distinguishing the very best educators from mediocre educators is self-awareness. Excellent educators possess an uncanny knack for knowing exactly how they are perceived by the students, staff, and parents with whom they interact. Less successful educators often lack an awareness of how they are perceived by students, parents, and colleagues.

In the classroom, excellent teachers actively monitor students throughout the lesson. They check for understanding, move about the room, and engage students actively in the lesson. When they sense that they are not connecting or communicating effectively, they stop and adjust the lesson. Afterward, they will intentionally reflect on what went wrong and then address it honestly with students the following day. Less effective teachers, on the other hand, rarely self-monitor how their lessons are unfolding and to what level students are engaged. Typically, they plod through the lesson as planned and pick up the following day with a very similar plan, regardless of whether students have understood and/or mastered the learning objectives—assuming any were actually planned.

Not surprisingly, great administrators have similar self-awareness. Excellent leaders check in with those they serve, ask for feedback on how they come across, and act accordingly upon this feedback. When leading a staff meeting or a professional learning session, they reflect on how it went and modify subsequent sessions based on their self-evaluation, as well as input from attendees. Conversely, less effective administrators simply keep doing the same thing they have always done, not seeming to mind whether those they are leading are responding, engaging, or following their lead.

Excellent teachers and leaders know quite a bit about teaching, leadership, students, pedagogy, standards, assessment, and professional learning. More important than any of these topics, however, is the extent to which they truly know themselves—their own strengths, shortcomings, passions, interests, likes, dislikes, and how they are being received by the students, parents, or fellow educators with whom they interact. Many of these educators appear to intuitively know how they are coming across. The truth is, however, that they intentionally seek feedback from a variety of stakeholders and do so frequently and in a variety of ways. They send out annual or perhaps semi-annual formal surveys to all staff members if they are administrators, or to students and parents if they are teachers. They seek out individual students, parents, or staff members—who they know will be forthcoming—and ask for feedback on how they are doing. They are masters in the art of active listening—especially when they are trying to gain an understanding of how they are being perceived and how they can improve. They are keen observers in the moment, constantly moving about the school or classroom, actively scanning the classroom, hallway, or meeting room, making eye contact with everyone they meet, reading their body language, and checking in with those who seem unengaged to find out why.

Most importantly, they do not stop at merely asking for feedback and input—they act upon what they learn. When they receive praise for doing well, they may quietly celebrate such feedback while continuing to work to get even better. When they learn that something they have said or done did not go as planned or, worse yet, resulted in a damaged relationship, they work to do better the next time and seek out affected parties to offer a sincere apology.

> ## One thing all excellent educators know about themselves is that they will never know it all.

Educators who know the way know themselves—inside and out. They are brutally honest with themselves when things go wrong, and take pride when things go well. In either scenario, they commit to moving forward tomorrow, doing better than they did today. One thing all excellent educators know about themselves is that they will never know it all; therefore, they seek out others who can help them learn and grow. Finally, although they intentionally work to improve in areas they find themselves lacking, they are even more passionate about improving the areas in which they are already strong. They understand that building off their strengths will take them as far as, or further than, slight improvements in any single area of deficit. Educators who are intimately in tune with their professional selves know what they are good at, what they are not so good at, how they can get better, who can help them get better, and how to seek out honest feedback to equip them to do so.

Know Your Stuff

Excellent people in any career possess a thorough knowledge about their chosen field. We would not visit doctors or dentists who did not know their area of medicine inside and out. We expect these professionals to continue learning throughout their careers, keeping current with new and emerging best practices. The same holds true for attorneys, real estate agents, or pharmacists we might consult. In each instance, we expect to be working with highly competent professionals who study, research, attend ongoing learning events, and seek out others in their professional networks and organizations with the intent of continually improving in their area of expertise.

Excellent people in any career possess a thorough knowledge about their chosen field.

It is equally important for educational professionals to know all aspects about their specific roles and the "science" behind it. Sometimes, however, the importance of actively seeking out educators who stand out in terms of their content knowledge and expertise gets downplayed when making hiring decisions. To be clear, we think the "art" of education is every bit as important (if not more so) than the "science" of education. That said, a strong foundation of knowledge and a keen intellect are non-negotiable attributes for excellence. In fact, there is not a single truly excellent school administrator we know who is not intimately aware of best practices in school leadership. Likewise, we have yet to meet any superior classroom teachers who are not also experts in the topics they are teaching.

Outstanding school principals and other administrators have studied at length to learn as much as possible about best practices in leadership, reading and researching a wealth of literature relating not only to school leadership, but also organizational leadership in general. In addition to earning advanced degrees in educational leadership, they continue learning by reading books, journal articles, blog posts, and a wide variety of other materials to stay current with emerging trends and to expand their knowledge base. They attend formal and informal professional learning events, ranging from local edcamps to regional and national conferences. They connect with leaders around the globe through Twitter and other social media platforms to learn about successes leaders are experiencing elsewhere in an effort to replicate such successes. The best classroom teachers exhibit the same zest for learning about their own content. We know some amazing math teachers, science teachers, English teachers, and kindergarten teachers. All of these teachers share many traits in common; however, a starting point for their excellence is that they know the content they are teaching, as well as best practices in pedagogy. Moreover, they never reach a point where they feel they know it all; as a result, they continually seek out new ways to learn even more.

Another trait shared by both administrators and teachers who stand out is that they do not limit their learning to a narrow scope of skills focused solely on their current role. For example, many excellent science teachers often spend hours studying how to become better at teaching reading and writing in the field of science because they know that, in the real world, scientists read and write frequently. Rather than adopting an all-too-common attitude of, "I'm not an English teacher," they commit to teaching their students to read and write like scientists. Similarly, school and district administrators do not limit their quest for knowledge to best practices in leadership. As the "lead learners" of their school or district, they intentionally seek to become well versed in any number of areas, from special education law, to social/emotional learning, to the 4 C's of twenty-first-century learning. They take the stance that they must learn not only *how* to lead, but also know *what* to lead. For that reason, they are constantly on the lookout for new areas of study which might improve the school or district they are leading.

Obviously, all teachers and administrators possess a certain amount of content knowledge related to their specific roles. In fact, most possess an extensive amount of such knowledge. However, educators who stand out as succeeding in knowing the way to excellence take learning to another level. When we ask others about such educators, we often hear them described using words such as, "zeal," "passion," "quest," and "curious" when talking about how much they know and continue to learn. They exhibit an obvious love for the kids they serve and the colleagues with whom they serve; their love for the content they are teaching or leading, and their desire for others to love it as much as they do, is equally evident. To achieve this goal, they leave no stone unturned in an effort to know their stuff.

People First

Although content knowledge is critically important, it is even more important to know your people. We have heard the following adage a million times by now and suspect you have as well: People don't care how much you know until they know how much you care. Truer words have never been spoken. Even the most erudite person in the world will never become excellent at his job if all he knows is the science behind his craft, but is bereft of knowledge about the people he is teaching or leading. Another oft repeated sentiment we have heard is that outstanding science (or math, Spanish, art, etc.) teachers don't teach science—they teach kids. Their content may happen to be science, but they are more focused on the human beings who are learning the content than on the content itself. As important as everything else is (including "knowing your stuff" as we just described), the very best educators know that people come first; everything else is a distant second.

The adage shared above is worth repeating, even if it is now for the 1,000,001st time: People don't care how much you know until they know how much you care. If this is true (and we fervently believe it is), teachers and leaders who do not care about the students they are teaching or the adults they are leading are simply doomed to failure. Ironically, we know of very few people in the entire field of education who do NOT care about their students or colleagues. In fact, the minuscule percentage of non-caring educators serving in our schools simply need to be counseled to seek another profession; we will never be able to make them care. A more sizable minority of educators DO sincerely care about the people with whom they interact on a daily basis, but do not always show it. For some, this perception of indifference may be by design; in others, it may be unintentional. Regardless, caring about others without showing them that you care is only slightly better than not caring at all. We must make it a priority to clearly show we care about the students, parents, and staff we serve. The most basic way to show you care is to actively and intentionally seek ways to truly know the people you are teaching and leading. The most successful education professionals go out of their way to know as much as possible about the people they are trying to engage, inspire, and empower.

Superstar teachers do everything in their power to know the students assigned to their classrooms. They care about the students they teach almost as much as they care about their own family members and friends. They learn about their interests, their hopes, their fears, their dreams, what they excel at, and what they are not so great at. They know about their lives outside of school, including their families, hobbies, schedules, and responsibilities. They even go the extra mile by occasionally attending a sporting event or fine arts event in which their students are participating. The more they know about the students they teach, the better they can connect and empathize with them and, ultimately, teach them—about learning standards, yes, but also about life. The same holds true, of course, for school leaders. They actively seek to understand the staff members they serve. What great teachers want to know about kids is what great leaders want to know about teachers: their passions, likes, dislikes, strengths, weaknesses, family, hobbies, personality traits, and work habits.

The funny thing is, we all have the ability to get to know our students and colleagues really well. Unfortunately, some educators view this aspect of their job as unimportant, claiming that, with all they are expected to do, they simply don't have time to learn about their students as people, instead of seeing them "just" as students. In contrast, the very best among us intentionally make time for this because they understand that they will never be able to do all that they are supposed to do if they do not first get to know the people they are charged with teaching.

The best educators put people first!

It is true that educators who succeed in "knowing the way" to excellence know their stuff. It is even more important that they know their people, whether that refers to students in their classroom or staff in their building. For years, Todd has used a simple phrase that anyone who has heard him speak remembers: It's people, not programs. Programs are never the problem and are never the solution; people are always the problem, and they are always the solution. Those who are the problem tend to be those who do not know and understand the people with whom they interact. Those who tend to be the solution are keenly aware that nothing matters more than knowing and caring about others—most importantly, students. The best educators put people first!

Non-Negotiables

Great teachers and leaders are collaborative professionals who tend to invite a "voice and choice" culture. Their students and staff members have a significant role both in setting goals and determining how to go about achieving them. At the same time, these great educators adhere to certain non-negotiables to ensure that everyone succeeds in completing the journey. They tend to be seen as fun, cheerful, supportive, and kind human beings. But make no mistake about it: These people are driven, focused professionals who are serious about their work. Because of this intentional focus on success and excellence, master teachers and administrators establish specific, non-negotiable parameters regarding the work ahead, including what the work is and how they will—collectively—approach it. Educators who believe in equity for all and are driven by empathy and compassion for others derive their non-negotiables from a fundamental core belief system whose decisions come from the heart. Decisions manifest themselves from an inner core which allows them to remain fair, consistent, and most importantly, to preserve the dignity of others when making decisions. Such teachers and leaders operate under a students-first mindset as opposed to an adult-centered mindset. As such, they always begin with the question, "How will this decision or action advance the well-being of the student(s)?"

Great teachers and leaders adhere to a loose-tight philosophy when working with kids and colleagues. They have what might be considered rigid expectations for what success will look like, yet they allow for, and even encourage, a great deal of autonomy in how individuals achieve certain goals. In the classroom, great teachers make it crystal clear from the first day of the school year what the non-negotiable expectations are for student behavior and work habits. Knowing what it will take for students to reach their fullest potential, these teachers communicate their expectations to their students individually and collectively. Although they allow for some group decisions regarding acceptable behaviors and work habits, these educators do not shy away from openly sharing their non-negotiables, frequently reinforcing them, and consistently holding all students accountable for adhering to these expectations. As always, what works for the best teachers in their classrooms also works for the best school administrators in their schools and districts, in which they also establish non-negotiables for how the adults in the building will conduct their work and the ways in which they will treat students and each other.

Great teachers and leaders are innovators who encourage risk taking and are always open to new ideas. By fostering a culture of "Yes" in their classrooms and schools, they empower others to take chances and try new things in order to create something great. They also see the value of failure, letting others know that it is OK to F.A.I.L. as a First Attempt In Learning. Highly qualified and highly effective, these educators have a clear sense of what success looks like, as well as what works and what does not in attempting to achieve it. As a result, they are not afraid to establish clear guidelines for students and staff with whom they interact. They know the way—the direction—they want their classroom, school, or district to go. They know what success looks like and what the end goals are. They communicate these clearly and consistently to all with whom they work. They also realize they

Great teachers and leaders are innovators who encourage risk taking and are always open to new ideas.

will never achieve these goals if they do not first establish clear expectations about general classroom, school, and district standards, letting everyone know at the outset not only what these non-negotiables are, but also why they matter. Of course, once they share what they know about where they are going, how they will get there, and why it matters, they then set about modeling their expectations on a daily basis. This modeling behavior is closely related to behaviors discussed later in this book in the section we call Go the Way.

Know When to Say No

One risk inherent to effective and efficient educators is that if they are not careful, they may end up trying to do too much. In addition to their primary job responsibilities related to classroom instruction or leading a school community, they are often asked to serve in a variety of other ways, from leading committee work and serving on district task forces to coaching sports teams and sponsoring student activities. With a focus on continual improvement, they often choose to engage in a wide variety of professional endeavors during their free time, whether that means pursuing advanced degrees and certifications, writing blog posts, or connecting with their P^{2}LN through Twitter or during Saturday edcamps. Although they tend to do much more than many of their less successful colleagues, they also know that they simply cannot and should not try to do it all. Thus, they intentionally say "no" when they feel they are overextended or are being asked to participate in work they feel is not the most important work they could be doing at the present time.

Balance is incredibly important although, at times, it seems like an impossible goal. Excellent teachers and leaders are regularly pulled in a million different directions, often simultaneously. One way they strive to maintain a balance in their personal and professional lives is by forcefully (though respectfully) saying "no" to certain requests and opportunities. They realize that every time they say "yes" to one thing, they are saying "no" to something else. Because they know themselves and their priorities, they know they must make the most productive choices in regard to their time, energy, and goals. They may even consciously ask themselves, "If I say 'yes' to this, what will I be saying 'no' to?" A classroom teacher who says "yes" to serving on another district-wide task force may be saying "no" to attending after-school events with students or exercising at home. She may still say "yes" if the work is urgent and important enough, but she intentionally considers what this new commitment will mean in terms of other personal and/or professional commitments.

If you have a host of important priorities, you have no important priorities.

We knew one busy principal who, because he was so effective and efficient, was constantly asked to do even more by his superintendent. Since he was very motivated and wanted to help in any way he could, his initial impulse was to say "yes." Over time, he realized that not everything he was saying "yes" to was focused on the work most critical to his own success and the success of the school he was leading. He reached a point where he thought carefully before committing to taking on any new assignment. When his superintendent asked him to lead yet another initiative, he reflected on whether it was the right work at the right time, and if he was the person best equipped to lead the work. When his private answer was "no" to these questions, he responded to his superintendent by respectfully and honestly saying, "I can do this if you really need me to, but what do you want me to stop doing or put off for now while I focus on this?" He then shared his list of current priorities and calendar events, letting the superintendent know that something would have to go if this new work were to be done. His superintendent, who was an excellent leader herself, realized the folly of asking this particular school leader to take on even more work that was not the most important work for him to be doing at the time. She respected his honesty and asked someone who was less busy and more suited to the task at hand.

Teachers and school administrators are extremely busy professionals. Like busy professionals in any field, they run the risk of taking on too much. They also run the risk of taking on a "new thing" without saying goodbye to an "old thing" and, in the process, run the risk of juggling more and more initiatives and responsibilities with each passing school year. Excellent educators, whether they are serving in the classroom or serving as school administrators, know when to say "no." They periodically "weed the garden" of all they do, intentionally taking time to stop doing things that are no longer of critical importance. This allows them to tend to the growth of the most urgent and important ideas and initiatives they have planted. Effective school and district leaders regularly engage the school community in a transparent discussion aimed at prioritizing collective points of emphasis, agreeing on what they must *start*, *stop*, and *continue* doing. When they agree, after careful deliberation, that specific current programs must *continue* and also agree to *start* one new program, they do so only after identifying what it is they are going to *stop* doing to ensure that all of the initiatives will succeed. The reality is that if you have a host of important priorities, you have no important priorities. The very best teachers and school leaders continually examine what their core priorities are, and then make sure those are the efforts that receive the bulk of their focus and effort.

The Gift of Confidence

Successful classroom teachers and building leaders are not cocky or arrogant, but they do have tremendous confidence in themselves, fervently believing in their work and in their ability to do it. Like all human beings, they occasionally experience brief episodes of self-doubt, but they quickly regroup and refocus on their mission and how best to accomplish it. Knowing how important self-confidence is to their own success, they aspire to instill this same sense of confidence in students they teach and staff members they lead. In fact, they know that confidence is the greatest gift they can give students or staff members they serve.

Teachers who instill confidence within their students tend to believe in what Jonathan Saphier calls "effort-based ability":

> *Educators who believe in effort-based ability believe that all students can do rigorous academic work at high standards, even if they are far behind academically and need a significant amount of time to catch up. Educators who carry this belief into practice are not unrealistic about the obstacles they and their students face. They simply have not given up. And we know for sure that they will get results if they translate this belief into appropriate practice.[1]*

Such teachers know that the single most important variable impacting whether a student can accomplish something is that student's belief that he can accomplish it. They also know that the variable most likely to affect a student's belief in their own ability is the teacher's belief in their ability. If the teacher communicates her confidence in the student's ability, the student will have more confidence in his own ability. One thing excellent teachers can do to promote self-confidence is to communicate and demonstrate that they believe in the ability of others to achieve at high levels. They communicate on a daily basis that being smart is "something you can get," and not simply something with which you are born.

The single most important variable impacting whether a student can accomplish something is that student's belief that he can accomplish it.

School leaders also work intentionally to give the gift of confidence to teachers with whom they work. They do this in a variety of ways. They visit classrooms regularly, and follow up on informal visits by writing short notes complimenting teachers on something they saw while there. They encourage teachers to visit each other's classrooms and to share their expertise openly with one another. They see amazing things happening in classrooms and encourage the teachers doing these things to blog and tweet about them. They encourage teachers to attend professional learning events and submit proposals to present at such events. They thank and praise teachers—privately and publicly—for doing work above and beyond the call of duty aligned with their mission. They actively seek honest opinions about pressing issues facing teachers and act on this advice. They consistently communicate that the single most important variable impacting student performance is high-quality teaching and highlight exemplary teaching practices in a variety of ways.

In schools that value the concept of this effort-based ability to which Saphier alludes, teachers and administrators constantly remind students and themselves of three crucial messages:[2]

1. The work we are doing is important.

2. You (We) can do it.

3. I (We) will not give up on you (each other).

It is not uncommon to learn that excellent educators have had someone in their own lives who believed in them and consistently communicated to them that they were able, valuable persons who could and would do great things (often, the encourager was also an educator). Such teachers never forget this and pay it forward to the students they are teaching or the colleagues they are leading today.

If we consistently send these messages to all students and educators in our schools regarding our belief in effort-based ability, our students and staff will begin to believe in themselves and become motivated members of our school culture based on aspiration and responsibility. Why? Because someone cares about them. Someone wants them to succeed. They know what to work on in order to do well, they know what good work looks like, and they know where their current performance is in relation to the goal. They know how to exert effort, and they believe it would be worthwhile to do well. They believe they are able to do well thanks, in part, to receiving the gift of confidence from an excellent teacher or school leader.

Believing that we each have innate capacity that can be grown is a foremost tenet of successful educators. Obviously, we all are born with innate skills and abilities, but it is effective effort that is the primary determinant of achievement. Excellent teachers and leaders who know the way know that confidence is a gift that keeps on giving, and they do everything they can to instill self-confidence within their students and colleagues.

Plan for Success

An intentional plan for success guides great teachers and administrators in their achievements. Whether planning for successful school improvement, classroom instruction, or district-wide innovation, they honestly assess their current reality and then plan strategic next steps for success. They establish goals of all kinds, including short- and long-term goals, as well as district, school, classroom, and individual goals. They establish the long-term strategies to achieve their goals and experience continuous improvement. Additionally, they determine the specific, short-term techniques they will use to ensure the strategies are within reach. They hold fast to ambitious hopes and dreams for the communities they serve, but move beyond merely hoping and dreaming for success by planning for these hopes and dreams to become reality.

For many educators, time seems to be the enemy of the hopes and dreams they have for themselves as educators, as well as for their students and colleagues. The misconception is that if only we had more time, then we could get to everything necessary to make our dreams come true.

The good news is that time is a constant for all; we each have sixty seconds every minute, sixty minutes every hour, twenty-four hours every day, and seven days every week available to us. Excellent teachers and leaders are faced with the exact same time constraints facing everyone, yet rather than complain about it, they do something about it: They plan their time well. Knowing that time is precious and limited, they make the most of every second they have, whether that second is spent working with a small group of kids in a classroom, coaching a fellow teacher on a new teaching technique, or observing a staff member teaching and then providing feedback. Regardless of what excellent educators are doing with any given second of the day, the way they are spending it has likely been carefully planned out in advance. In a great teacher's classroom and in a great principal's school, very little happens at random. Great teachers and school leaders have a plan for everything they do. Furthermore, when things do not go as planned, they take the time to reflect on what occurred and what they will do differently next time to affect a better outcome.

Even though highly effective principals and teachers intentionally plan for almost all that occurs in their schools and classrooms, they may make it seem as if events are unfolding at random. Oftentimes, what is a surprise to students in a classroom or staff members at a faculty meeting are events that have been meticulously planned in advance by a strategic teacher or administrator. Unless we are the ones doing the planning, activities seem to roll out almost effortlessly. In reality, there is an intentional plan behind each and every activity. When Jeff was living in a small coastal community, he attended services at the same church every Sunday for seven consecutive years. One Sunday, the music minister stood to tell everyone which hymn they were about to sing and added something that surprised Jeff: "After singing today's hymn, we will have sung every song in the hymnal since I arrived here as the music minister." Even though Jeff had attended services at this church every single Sunday for seven consecutive years, he had no idea that they had worked their way through every song in the hymnal or that the music minister had an apparent strategy behind what he was doing in his leadership role. Many parishioners marveled when they learned there was actually a rhyme and reason to the songs he selected each week. Likewise, although the activities may seem random to observers, in districts, schools, and classrooms, excellent educators intentionally design learning and leading opportunities. Because they start by asking themselves why they are doing what they are doing, they have a long-term strategy for success and a purpose in mind for every event they schedule.

The excellent teachers and principals we have observed through the years are planners. They plan and execute daily lessons, units of study, staff meetings, team meetings, celebrations, school assemblies, and even disaster drills. All of these activities are intentionally designed to purposefully call on students and/or staff to engage in a wide variety of tasks and behaviors that are aligned to specific intended outcomes. These teachers and leaders differentiate their plans for the students or staff with whom they are working, believing that beginning where indi-vidual people are, rather than with a prescribed series of actions that ignores human variance, is more likely to result in accomplishing the mission. Our kids and staff members are unique learners with unique needs. As mentioned earlier, we must work to know everything we can about them. Such knowledge allows us to meet them where they are and help them get to the intended destination. How each individual gets there and how long each spends at stops along the way can vary. That is not only OK, it is actually a good and normal thing. Learning can be a messy and difficult process, but then again, most things worth doing are not clean and easy.

> ## Learning can be a messy and difficult process, but, then again, most things worth doing are not clean and easy.

Educators who succeed in knowing the way to excellence dedicate a significant portion of their limited and precious time to planning for success. They know that the more time they spend planning on the front end, the more time they can save on the back end. Spending hours planning lessons or planning for an upcoming professional learning workshop is not the most glamorous aspect of their jobs, but they realize that if they fail to invest fully in the planning process, they will never achieve the results they seek. They know, too, that seeing students or colleagues learning and growing is well worth the effort of intentional planning.

TEACH 4, LEAD 4, LEARN 4

Teachers and leaders with whom we have worked, and who stand out as truly excellent, exhibit a clear pattern of knowing the way in all that they do. They know what their mission is, both as individual educators and as part of a larger school community. They know themselves inside and out, and they regularly seek feedback to understand how they can improve. They know all aspects of the content relevant to their specific role as an educator. They intentionally get to know the people with whom they work, taking time to learn their strengths, interests, hopes, and dreams. Although they allow for and encourage a great deal of autonomy and choice from the people they are charged to teach and lead, they set high expectations for what is non-negotiable in their district, school, or classroom. They are capable of saying "no" when demands on their time threaten to push them too far out of balance or cause them to veer too far from their chosen path. They know that confident people are more likely to be successful people, so they not only possess a calm self-confidence, but also seek to give the gift of confidence to the students and staff they serve. Finally, they know that making their hopes and dreams a reality requires them to intentionally plan their goals, strategies, techniques, and use of time.

During the past several decades, we have met hundreds of educators who stand as beacons in the area of knowing the way to excellence. Some serve in classrooms, while others serve as building administrators. Still others serve in other leadership roles in schools or districts. We have witnessed master educators exhibiting some or all of what we have written about in this chapter. Thankfully, they have taken the time to share just a bit about how they know the way in their current roles.

Teach 4

The following four teachers exemplify what it means to Know the Way. They explain why being intentional about knowledge matters.

1. **Pernille Ripp (@pernilleripp)** is a middle-school teacher, speaker, author, blogger, and passionate advocate for education. She is widely respected for her knowledge about her kids, as well as the content she teaches. She is highly regarded around the world for her expertise in the area of literacy. Pernille *knows her stuff.*

As a new teacher, I realized I did not know a lot about all of the subject areas I was about to teach. After all, they can only cram so much information into your head in college, no matter what the quality of your education program is. While it scared me that I knew so little, I thought that the path toward more content knowledge was rather simple: Teaching more would equal learning more. Couple that with the district-mandated professional development, and I was sure I was set. After all, if my district was OK with that amount of further learning, then I would be as well. Now, I know that although we do get better with more experience, we must go beyond learning through osmosis or professional development picked for us by others. Becoming connected not only to other educators through social media, but also within my own district, has made me realize just how much I still need to learn about teaching reading well. So I am on a continuous quest to become better, not because I have to, but because I see the major impact it has on the type of learning my students engage in. Whenever I learn more about reading, I am quickly reminded just how little I still know, and so the quest for content knowledge continues from book, to conversation, to conference, to presentation, and back to my students. Because it is not just the professional sources that are available to us as we further our content knowledge that should shape what we know; what the students need should also drive our learning. And you will not know that until you ask them. My students are part of my professional development; their truths about how I can become a better teacher for them is what spurs me onward so that, perhaps one day, I can look back and realize that while I never learned it all, I certainly kept on trying.

2. Kirk Humphreys (@Kirk_Humphreys) is a middle-school math teacher in Deerfield, Illinois. Kirk is widely known for his colorful personality, his ability to connect with kids and colleagues, and his meticulous planning. Kirk is a leader in the area of the flipped-classroom approach to teaching and learning. Kirk knows the importance of *planning for success.*

Knowing the students who walk through my classroom is the first key to their success. By knowing each individual learner, I am better able to plan lessons designed to meet them where they are and take them to their next level. With the flipped-classroom approach, students watch videos of the lessons whenever they choose. Class time is spent on collaborative activities that delve deeper into the concepts from the videos. Each day, students start class by explaining the concepts learned from the videos. Students, who are in charge, call on each other while I observe what is happening. Students correct each other's mistakes, make their own problems and, in their own words, show how well the material has been learned. Students are given ownership, and I am simply on the sidelines observing. Using this knowledge, I can get an instant snapshot of how well students have mastered the concepts. This allows more questioning from the students and from me. As students work, I am able to have conversations with each student or group of students. I ask questions such as, "What can you show me that proves you've mastered the concept..." or, "How would this concept be explained to others who do not understand what is being learned?" to help guide each student on their individual path for learning. From there, modifications are made for each student. Students are able to choose the pace at which they work and compete with themselves, not with each other. With constant formative assessments, I am able to know exactly where students are in understanding the concepts. This approach to teaching requires a great deal of upfront planning, but it is worth it!

3. Madeline Whitaker (@MWhitaker_Ed) is a third-grade teacher in Springfield, Missouri. Part of her success comes from the extra efforts she makes to know her students both as learners and as unique human beings. Madeline knows the power of *people first*.

> *As an elementary-school teacher, it can be easy for me to view my students as just "students." Although knowing them as students is an important aspect of my job as an instructor and facilitator of their learning, I take specific steps to be sure I get to know them as true individuals: members of families, communities, and cultures all their own. Without the understanding of their individuality, it is impossible to build true relationships or a classroom community. One strategy I use to grow this is to take one lunch a week and invite students to my classroom just to chat about what is important to them that day. Sometimes the topic is friends and family, while other times we discuss the latest video game or TV show that has piqued their interest. I also make sure my students have daily opportunities to "free write" as an additional way for them to express their personalities. They can share these pieces with me online or in paper form, which provides another avenue for me to experience my students' inner dialogue, personal experiences, and wild creativity. These conversations help remind me that, just like me, my students have interests that may not fit into the traditional "school" mold, but these interests are important glimpses into their personal spirit. They help shed light on what makes each student unique, which helps to cultivate the relationships upon which great classrooms are built.*

4. Kayla Delzer (@TopDogTeaching) is a third-grade teacher and technology champion in North Dakota. She has become known around the world for the work she has done in her classroom; moreover, her students have become known around the world for what they are doing in her classroom. Kayla knows the importance of empowering her students by giving them the *gift of confidence*.

As a third-grade classroom teacher, one of my emphases is to construct situations where my students can really shine and cultivate confidence in themselves and one another. Our classroom mantra that hangs high on our wall in large letters is, "Everyone teaches. Everyone learns." Every single day, students get up on our stage to perform and teach whole-group lessons to their peers. They feel empowered, significant, and, most importantly, confident. My students also have complete control of where they sit in our classroom during independent or collaborative work time, as they don't have assigned seats from day one. By giving my students power in our classroom and several different flexible seating options, they are comfortable and confident to choose seating that helps them learn best. I have actually found that the more power I give up in our classroom, the more power I get back. Lastly, my students gain confidence by sharing their daily classroom activities with thousands of followers using our student-led social media account, @topdogkids. They garner instant feedback from a global audience that is invested in and supports their learning, and my students feel their work has real significance. As a classroom teacher, giving my students the gift of confidence is one of the most critical contributions I can provide.

Lead 4

The following four educators currently serve in educational leadership roles. When you read their comments, you'll understand why we believe they stand out as exemplars for Knowing the Way:

1. **Neil Gupta (@drneilgupta)** is director of secondary education for Worthington City Schools, Ohio. As a district-level administrator, Neil continually receives requests from various stakeholders who want him to invest in new programs and initiatives. Although Neil is always open to new ideas, he also is keenly aware of the district's focus on their mission. He is careful not to say "yes" to something that may cause the

district to veer from its path to ongoing growth and improvement. As a successful leader, Neil *knows when to say "no."*

Lead learners are masters of the "Hedgehog Principle" Jim Collins references in his book Good to Great[3] *to show the power of maintaining a hyper-focus on what is most critical to success. Unlike the wily fox, which moves in many directions, the hedgehog moves in one path without being swayed or distracted. This means that hedgehogs not only know where to go, but they know where not to go. And they have no pretenses, excuses, or reasons for their single-mindedness other than that the other stuff doesn't move them towards the goal or desired outcome they need to work on. As a leader, I work with other district- and building-leader teams to identify the needs of our students and create aligned goals. We design action plans based on these goals and communicate and articulate them throughout the district. Having these goals and plans developed and monitored on a regular basis allows us, like the hedgehog, to know where we are going. More importantly, this focus provides us with the strength and clarity to identify which things are not connected to the goals, so we can confidently say "no" to those distractions. We are faced with an infinite number of initiatives we can choose to implement; knowing which to say "yes" to is, of course, important. Knowing which to say "no" to may be even more important so we do not lose our focus.*

2. **Ben Gilpin (@benjamingilpin)** is an elementary-school principal in Spring Arbor, Michigan. In addition to serving as principal, Ben is also an avid long-distance runner. In both roles, Ben takes intentional actions to monitor his performance and reflect on where he is doing well and where he needs to improve. In his reflection below, Ben makes an analogy between the two as a way to describe the importance of *knowing thyself.*

As the sweat dripped off of my chin, I could feel my heart thumping. In ten seconds, the gun would fire and the race would start. In my mind I was confident, excited, and optimistic. BANG! We were off. I started out like a shot and was among the race leaders. Then, we encountered a large hill around the two-mile mark. As I crested the top, I quickly assessed how I felt and realized I was not going to finish among the leaders. The lead pack was pulling away, and I still had nearly three miles left in the race. I found my more natural pace and began to work towards the finish line. That day was a rude awakening. I was getting good at learning about myself. I knew I was a strong starter, but I also understood my body and I learned that heat and hills hurt me and that I needed to pace myself properly. It was then that I really began to grow as a runner. I was honest with myself and it allowed me to get better.

I relate growth as a runner to my understanding of myself as an educational leader. Before I can grow, I need to reflect and understand what my strengths and weaknesses are. The mistake I often see from fellow leaders is false belief. Leaders can be stubborn and believe they are gifted in all areas. The true mark of a strong leader is humility. Knowing that you are not the master of all things will endear you to others. The mile-two hill smacked me in the face and quickly taught me my reality. Leaders face the proverbial mile-two hill each day. Will you be a reflective leader and assess your strengths and weaknesses? Try listening before talking to others. Embrace surveys from staff and community. Ultimately, be willing to be brutally honest with yourself. Then the forward movement can truly begin. Knowing yourself is a key characteristic, in my opinion, of all educators. As Aristotle noted, "Knowing yourself is the beginning of all wisdom."

3. **Nick Polyak (@npolyak)** is a superintendent at Leyden Community High School District 212 in suburban Chicago, Illinois.

As superintendent, he makes many short- and long-term decisions. He stresses the importance of keeping in mind two important questions when deciding the next steps for the district he leads. Nick knows the importance of *starting with why, then where*.

We operate by a very simple, overarching premise when making decisions: What's best for the kids? As the superintendent, I often describe the role and responsibility we have in schools as a two-filter test. Our community sends us two of their most precious assets: their tax dollars and their children. When considering important questions, I always ask myself two questions:

1. Is this what's best for the kids?

2. Is this a responsible use of our local resources?

If the answer to both questions is yes, then it is likely a smart decision to make as a school leader. This has been an important mindset for me when considering questions of equity in our school district. One example: We are a 1:1 school district that provides a Google Chromebook at no charge for all 3,500 students. We also identify students without Internet access at home and we provide a wireless hotspot so they can have equal access to connectivity both in and out of school. We believe those tools are part of what students need to be college, career, and life ready. Although the cost is significant, we provide these tools because it is what's best for the kids.

4. **Maureen Miller (@mmiller112)** is a director of technology in Winnetka, Illinois. In her role as a technology leader for a school district, Maureen works to support all staff as they face seemingly endless changes in instructional practices. Knowing that—like students—the various staff members she leads are at all different points on the technology learning curve, Maureen differentiates her support and allows for a great deal of choice among the staff in how and what they learn when it comes to technology. However, she also *communicates her*

non-negotiables—the expectations she has for all staff. She knows that it is important to allow for individual differences while also expecting a certain level of commitment from all.

It's never enough to just keep doing what you are doing; the world is changing much too fast to merely keep pace. As a leader, you have to be willing to put yourself out there, make connections, model best practices, and help others to do the same. These are my non-negotiables for those I lead. It's not possible to ever stop learning; it's not okay to settle for "good enough." Every day, you must work harder to be better than yesterday.

In our district, we understand that some staff members are further along than others when it comes to the area I am directly responsible for leading: technology. Although I do not expect every staff member to get to the same point at the same time when focusing on technology, I do have a non-negotiable expectation that every staff member moves from her Point A to her personal Point B. Another non-negotiable I hold myself accountable for is to always keep connecting with others as a way to grow and learn. I don't know what I'd do if I weren't connected to so many smart people through my professional learning network, both in person and online. I learn from my PLN every day, and I'm a better leader because of them.

Because others have always been there to support and encourage me throughout my career, it's important for me to give back. When I see a spark in someone, I will always work hard to flame that spark and help that person reach their goals. Often, our future leaders can do more than they think they can. It's up to us to encourage them to go for it and take risks, and we must be there to support them along the way. I lead because I love learning. I lead because I love helping others to learn. I lead because I want to encourage and support future leaders. To succeed, I need to be patient, encouraging, and flexible. At the same time, I must communicate what is not negotiable for everyone in our district once we have committed to any new technology.

Learn 4

Here are four resources/ideas/action steps we recommend exploring to further develop yourself and others relating to the standard we call Knowing the Way:

1. **Create a personal mission statement.** In the classic book *The 7 Habits of Highly Effective People*, Stephen Covey wrote, "Writing or reviewing a mission statement changes you because it forces you to think through your priorities deeply, carefully, and to align your behavior with your beliefs."[4] We agree that writing a personal mission statement can be a powerful and enduring activ-

Personal Mission Statements of 5 Famous CEOs

ity, and we encourage all educators to do so. There are any number of methods for crafting your personal mission statement as an educator. Our simple approach is to focus on questions such as the following:

*   Why do schools exist?

*   Why do we need teachers and leaders?

*   Why did I enter the education profession? What were my hopes and dreams then? What are they now?

*   What is my fundamental purpose in my current role?

A personal mission statement is a philosophy or creed that focuses on why you do what you do each day as an educator. Although mission statements among educators around the globe may sound quite similar overall, your personal mission statement should also describe your unique purpose and passion as an educator. It should summarize the talents and qualities you have and those you want to develop. It would identify what you want to accomplish in your role and what contributions you desire to make on behalf of the students and/or staff you serve.

Personal mission statements can become the basis for making daily decisions. When we have a choice to make, we can consider which option gets us closer to accomplishing our ultimate goal, our mission. Everything we do either helps us fulfill our mission and accomplish goals, or moves us further away from doing so. When we make decisions based on our personal mission statements, we tend to never regret it. Your mission statement may change slightly over time, which is completely acceptable and even a good thing. Feel free to modify it periodically based on new learning, new experiences, new awareness, and evolutions in your thinking over time. Check out this short article, "Personal Mission Statements of 5 Famous CEOs (And Why You Should Write One Too)" for further ideas.[5]

2. Read "A 4-Part System for Getting to Know Your Students" by Jennifer Gonzalez.[6] In this short blog post, Jennifer shares simple, yet powerful, ways to connect with the students we serve.

A 4-Part System for Getting to Know Your Students

3. Watch Simon Sinek's TED Talk about the importance of starting with *Why?*: "How Great Leaders Inspire Action."[7] Sinek maintains that very few people or organizations know why they do what they do. By "why," he means: What's your purpose? What's your cause? What's your belief? Why does your organization exist? Why do you get out of bed in the morning? And why should anyone care? He makes a compelling case for starting with "Why?"

How Great Leaders Inspire Action

4. **Watch "How To Write a Mission Statement that Doesn't Suck,"** a short video by Dan Heath.[8] Dan Heath provides a humorous—though accurate—look at what goes wrong with many mission statements. He offers inspiring examples, as well as less effective mission statements. He encourages the use of concrete language and answering the "Why?" in writing your mission statement.

How To Write a
Mission Statement
that Doesn't Suck

SHOW THE WAY

*That's what heroic stories do for us. They show us the way.
They remind us of the good we are capable of.*
—Sam Raimi

Although Mr. Raimi is referring, we suspect, to the stories he tells through the films he directs, his point is also worth considering for the purposes of this book. Excellent teachers and leaders use stories as well as their personal example to show the way. In doing so, they remind those they teach and lead of their abilities as students and fellow educators.

Educators who stand out as excellent teachers and leaders recognize that what others expect of them matters far less than what they expect of themselves. They have a sense of passion, a sense of purpose, and a sense of pride when it comes to their work and, more importantly, how they live their daily lives. They show the way by listening, serving, and investing their time in others. Excellent teachers and leaders are storytellers who never settle for the status quo, but paint a picture of a better future and share this vision with the students and educators they teach or serve alongside. These forward-thinking opti-mists then enlist others in their vision of a better tomorrow as they *show the way* to excellence.

DEFINING THE STANDARD: SHOWING THE WAY FOR EXCELLENCE

The second standard of teaching and leading for excellence exhib-ited by the genuine, caring, and servant-minded educators with whom we have worked is all about envisioning a better tomorrow and show-ing others how they can improve so that, collectively, they can attain that vision. What follows is a detailed description of this standard, but here's a brief definition of what it means to *Show the Way*: **Establishing a clear vision of future success and enlisting others in the vision by showing how each individual and team member can get better at what they do.**

STANDARD OF EXCELLENCE #2
Excellent Teachers and Leaders Show the Way

Excellent teachers and leaders show others in their districts, schools, departments, and classrooms where they are headed and how they can contribute to their future individual and collective success. They clearly communicate priorities and work to increase the capacity of those they teach and lead so that goals are achieved.

INDICATORS

- Builds consensus around a common set of values for running the district, school, department, or classroom
- Invites others to share in an exciting vision for the future
- Shows others how their long-term interests can be realized by enlisting in a common vision of future success

- Paints the "big picture" of what they aspire to accomplish as part of a team
- Communicates top district, school, department, and classroom priorities, as well as plans to grow and improve
- Articulates a vision for the students they serve and staff members with whom they serve
- Communicates a clear vision of the future on a consistent basis to various stakeholders
- Collaborates with various stakeholders for the purpose of ensuring success for students and staff
- Identifies and communicates what is working and what is not, both inside and outside the district, school, department, and classroom
- Spends time and energy making certain that people with whom they interact adhere to agreed-upon principles and standards
- Shares success stories and shows how these stories can inform and drive future success
- Celebrates students and staff whose behaviors contribute to a more positive future
- **Focuses on the question, "What do we hope to become as a district, school, department, or classroom?" and behaves in ways aligned to realizing this vision.**

Why It Matters

As described in Chapter Two, excellent educators begin their preparation for success by acquiring and exhibiting the necessary knowledge and skills related to their roles. It is not enough, however, to simply possess high levels of knowledge if we wish to make a profound impact beyond the four walls of one classroom or the boundaries of one school. Truly amazing teachers and leaders do not stop at improving themselves; they show others how they, too, can grow and get better and how, with a collective commitment, the entire school or district can achieve new heights. Such educators are risk takers who embrace change as both a challenge and an opportunity for growth.

One of the biggest challenges facing teachers and school leaders today is the constant and necessary need for *change*. The simple truth is great change begins with self-change. In other words, we cannot ask others to do what we are not willing to do ourselves if we want our classrooms and schools to reflect our high standards and expectations of excellence. No longer can we allow ourselves to get stuck in a fixed mindset that defines the role of what we do as, "It is what it is, and it's always been this way." If our intentions are to show others the way to a better tomorrow and inspire others to follow our lead, then we must create more opportunities for ourselves and for others to lead and inspire. We must tell our stories in ways that demonstrate how wonderful and important the education profession really is and how, together, we can reach higher and higher levels of performance. What others believe the job demands and how they see it depends on those of us teaching and leading them. No longer does school have to look like it has always looked, or be what others want it to be. Excellent educators take responsibility for their own behavior, including creating a collective vision of what they can become.

We must take initiative and be the *change*, not the *same*.

The finest teachers and leaders we know continue their journey on the path to excellence by showing others how to learn, how to plan for future success, how to effectively manage change, and how to move beyond the status quo. As important as it is to model the behaviors they seek, these educators realize they must first establish a long-term vision of the future that is clear, compelling, and attainable. Then, they must communicate how this exciting vision of the future can be accomplished.

Top-notch educators do not wait for change to happen to them. They proactively anticipate impending changes and make these changes work *for* them, rather than wasting energy working *against* change. We cannot paralyze ourselves because others are not doing the things that need to be done. We must take initiative and be the *change*, not the *same*. Our work is too important to settle for mediocre classrooms and schools, or practices that were "good enough" in the past. Excellent teachers and leaders know this, and as a result, they create a compelling vision of the future, enlist others in the vision, and invest in others by showing them the path to success.

What It Looks Like

20/20 Vision

A collaborative and team-oriented mindset drives excellent teachers and administrators to intentionally and consistently include their students or teachers in classroom, school, and district decisions. And although they welcome (and are not threatened by) input, they have a crystal-clear vision of what they intend to accomplish—in the next lesson, the next week, the next month, over the course of a school year, and even several years into the future. They inspire those they serve by sharing a vision of a better tomorrow. They clearly describe the possibilities and benefits, while taking time to explain why it is a realistic, credible, and attractive future for all. With that foundation, they invite others to join them on this journey.

At the start of any lesson or unit of study, great teachers show their students what they will know and be able to do upon completion. At the outset of any school year, great principals paint the picture of what the year will look like, including much of what will be accomplished by the end of the year. Like everyone else, these educators make many mistakes—and learn from these mistakes. Their ability to stay focused on definite end goals enables them to take risks and keep going when they encounter obstacles and challenges along the way. They are not shy about sharing where they intend to take others because they believe the goals they have set—once realized—will achieve ultimate excellence for those they serve. You might say they have perfect, 20/20 vision when it comes to what success looks like. Moreover, they are so passionate about this vision of a better tomorrow that *their* vision soon becomes a *shared* vision, collectively pursued by those in their presence.

Create a vision, and then be a living example of what it takes to achieve it.

Whenever Jimmy speaks with educators, he shares his observation that, unfortunately, "There is a lot of average out there." We implore you to shoot for amazing rather than average. One small, but powerful, way to rise above average is to insist on showing others the way by creating a vision and, equally as important, by being a living example of what it takes to achieve that vision. Excellence requires that we move beyond merely *telling* those we lead—whether students or staff—what we hope to become and what this shared vision looks like, to *showing* it—often and in a variety of ways. Like most things worth pursuing, showing can be challenging, and is certainly more difficult than simply telling others what we will do. Although we can learn certain techniques designed to show rather than tell and practice these techniques in our classrooms and meetings, showing a vision for a better tomorrow begins with something less tangible. It starts with an intuitive feeling on the part of the visionary educator, fueled by an unbridled passion. This passion is not something that can be feigned. Visionary leaders who succeed in inspiring others to participate in the vision are able to do so, in part, because of their genuine belief in and passion for the vision. They possess a gut instinct about "what can be," even in the face of a sometimes daunting "what actually is," and their energy, enthusiasm, and genuineness attracts others to their vision. They show the way by boldly and confidently (though never arrogantly) communicating what can be and then showing others—through their words, stories, actions, body language, support, and active listening—how, collectively, it will be accomplished.

One simple way they "show versus tell" is by specifically describing how individual lives will improve when the collective vision is realized. As a small, but specific, example, in classrooms led by teachers whose vision includes high levels of learning for all, students are motivated not by high test scores themselves but by what happens when they achieve high test scores. When students do well on assessments and show they have mastered core learning outcomes, any number of good things happen as a result. On the other hand, when scores on such tests are less than expected, many unfortunate consequences can occur, including the likelihood that schools will begin to focus even more on the tests, rather than on innovative teaching and learning practices. As Todd stated in his book *What Great Teachers Do Differently*, "Without success, tests become the school."[1] Excellent educators do not want their schools to become all about the tests; they have a loftier vision. As a result of this vision, such educators do not ignore or underestimate the impact mandated assessments can have on students, teachers, schools, and districts.

None of us entered the teaching profession because of our passion for standardized testing; however, the best educators waste neither their energy, nor their students' energy, by spending inordinate amounts of time complaining about such testing—even though they may well make their professional opinions known at the right time, the right place, and in a constructive manner that argues for what they perceive as right for students' learning and success. Instead, they go about their daily business of designing and delivering challenging and engaging learning experiences—which also, coincidentally, often optimize each child's chances for success on any mandated testing. They know that learning comes first and success on mandated testing is subordinate in importance to the learning. They also know, however, that their innovative, engaging instructional practices will likely result not only in student learning but also in success on required tests. In the process of going about their daily business of engaging students in learning-focused lessons, they show their students all the good that can happen when they master the intended objectives. Excellent educators do not believe in the value of testing more than others, but they are honest with themselves and realize they have a responsibility to teach students how to do well on state or provincial accountability measures without encroaching on the promise of teaching excellence.

In 1963, Dr. Martin Luther King, Jr. boldly proclaimed, "I have a dream." Note the pronoun use here: "I." Now, Dr. King was one of the most selfless and collaborative servant leaders in our nation's entire history and when we think of him, we think "we" rather than "I." Yet, the dream had to originate with the ultimate leader of the movement, not the masses. Once he communicated his powerful message as one man's dream, he then set about inspiring others to make it the nation's dream. Moreover, he did not simply tell others his dream; he showed what this ultimate vision would look like in reality at some point in the future. The imagery he employed in his famous speech, the personal examples he shared, and the stories he told painted a vivid picture of what racial equality would and should look like for all Americans. Although not usually as widely known as Dr. King's historic dream, each great leader or teacher has a vision, or a dream, for the work they do and how it can make a positive difference in the lives of those they serve. They show everyone they lead—in the classroom, school, or district—a vivid picture of what this exciting future looks like, and what it holds in store for them individually and as a community. They remain future-focused on this vision as they go about living in the present, exhibiting consistent behaviors aligned with the vision. Through their boundless energy, optimism, passion, and hope, they inspire others to share in the vision every step of the way; they know that without the commitment of others, it will never be achieved. Consequently, in addition to showing others an exciting vision of the future and enlisting them in this shared journey to greatness, excellent educators also show others different ways of achieving the desired results. Although they are unwavering in what they hope to become and accomplish as a school, district, or classroom community, they offer a great deal of choice along the way, showing those they lead multiple paths to take and various opportunities for participating.

Support Innovation

Dr. Martin Luther King, Jr. stands as one of our nation's most obvious examples of a man with a vision of a better tomorrow. His dream inspired millions to dream their own dreams. Likewise, in our schools and classrooms, excellent teachers and leaders are not the only ones with dreams. The students and staff they serve have dreams, too. Whether they achieve their dreams—or even take the first step of announcing their dreams—relies, to a large extent, on whether we inspire them to do so and whether we then support their efforts to dream, create, and make a difference.

Difference makers—in our schools and in our society as a whole—tend to be innovators. When we think of innovators in schools, we often think of the work George Couros has done in this area. George defines innovation as, "A way of thinking that creates something new and better." He reminds us that innovation can come about as invention (something totally new) or iteration (refining something already in place to make it new and improved).[2] Our highest-performing students and staff tend to be innovators who are not willing to wait for systemic transformation to happen. Instead, they choose to take matters into their own hands and innovate now—in their own classroom, school, or district. When students or teachers want to innovate, great educators reflexively respond by saying, "Yes! How can I support you?"

We agree with George that innovation is a mindset, rather than a skill set. The way we perceive changes and new ideas determines the extent to which such changes will be successful and such ideas will be implemented. If we perceive change, risk taking, and thinking differently as exciting challenges rather than disruptions to the status quo, we are more likely to innovate—and more likely to inspire innovative students and staff throughout our schools.

Great teachers empower students to use knowledge to change the world.

What our students learn in classrooms and what educators learn in any form of professional learning is not nearly as important as what they do with the learning they acquire. *Good* teachers help students learn facts so they can do well on tests and progress in school. *Great* teachers empower students to use the knowledge and skills they have acquired in the classroom to change the world. Unfortunately, not all students feel empowered to change the world, which is where great teachers come in. They challenge students to change the world and support them in doing so. One way teachers around the world are empowering and inspiring their students to innovate is by intentionally allowing for more student voice and choice in their classrooms. In many classrooms, something as simple as a weekly "Genius Hour" in which students pursue projects of interest and passion is changing the way students learn by actually doing something authentic and meaningful with their learning. We firmly believe that all students have the potential to become innovators and world changers. Some will rise to the occasion on their own. Many, however, need passionate, encouraging educators who support innovative thinking and acting on the part of their students. In a great teacher's classroom, innovation is embedded in the culture. The teacher's role in such classrooms is, at times, to employ innovative teaching techniques. More often, however, the teacher's role is to simply support innovative students who, by their very nature, wish to change the world. This support does not happen by accident. Excellent teachers anticipate the need to support innovation and plan for it just as carefully as they plan everything else that occurs in their classroom. They know that innovation may happen by chance occasionally, but is much more likely to occur when they actively plan for it, encourage it, and support it.

Students are not the only learners in schools, of course. Every adult in the building is a learner as well. Good teachers and administrators may make the time and effort to attend a professional learning workshop on any number of topics. Great teachers and administrators return to their schools after attending such workshops and make changes in their own practice to improve the lives of those they serve. If they learn of a better way to do something, they implement it. They never settle for "good enough" when they learn a better way. For example, a school leader who has seen the benefits of Genius Hour for students may realize that this approach to learning produces dividends for adults, too, and encourages personalized, professional learning for staff. Rather than offer one-size-fits-all training, great leaders support their staff members' efforts to learn what they want, when they want, and how they want.

Whether we are focusing on our kids or ourselves, we must always keep in mind that what we learn is not nearly as important as what we create from what we learn. Excellent teachers show this by supporting innovation—and innovators—in their classrooms. Excellent school leaders show this by doing everything in their power to support a culture of innovation throughout the school. Their vision is not to become the most innovative teacher or most innovative school leader; instead, their vision is to create a classroom, school, or district known for innovative teaching, learning, and leading for all. We often notice school or district vision statements that include some language related to producing "global citizens" or "productive members of the community." If the vision, or end goal, of school is to produce such outcomes, why wait? Choose to act now! Follow the lead of educators who provide those they serve with the time, support, and freedom they need to create a new and better tomorrow. Show the people you teach and lead that fulfilling the vision starts today.

Future-Focused While Attending to the Present

Do educators who excel at *showing the way* to a common vision of a better tomorrow focus on the future or attend to the present? Our short answer: yes. Excellent educators know that both are not only important, but possible. Like many things in education, the two are not mutually exclusive—if we have the proper mindset. Amazing educators possess such a mindset, knowing they must approach each and every day as a precious opportunity to make a long-term difference in the lives of the students and staff in their school communities.

Although it sounds obvious, we must remind ourselves to be there for others and, once there, to be fully present in the moment, without looking ahead to the next conversation, next lesson, next parent conference, or next school day. Teaching a lesson, leading a meeting, or holding a parent conference can all be opportunities for making a significant difference in the lives of others or for simply maintaining the status quo. Which outcome we get depends in part on the extent to which we sincerely attend to the present. Actively listening, seeking to understand, practicing empathy, carefully observing, and then adeptly adjusting based on what we are seeing, hearing, and understanding are just a few ways excellent educators attend to the present. They intentionally focus on today so that they will have a better sense of where next to move tomorrow, and the next day, and the day after that. Too often, we fall into the trap of having a plan for tomorrow and sticking with it, regardless of what happened today. The best leaders and teachers are certainly meticulous about daily, weekly, monthly, and yearlong planning, yet they continually adjust these plans based on the results they are getting each and every day. They possess the necessary ability to keep one eye on the future while keeping the other firmly focused on the here and now. They attend to the present so that they can better prepare themselves—and others—for the future.

Be fully present in the moment, without looking ahead to the next conversation, next lesson, next parent conference, or next school day.

Whenever we travel to the southern states, we enjoy the occasional visit to one of the ubiquitous Waffle House restaurants found there. If you have ever frequented a Waffle House, you know that they offer their hash browns in a variety of ways, including "scattered," "smothered," and "covered." Through careful (and delicious) research, we have detected a relationship between Waffle House hash browns and attending to the present in our schools. For instance, we have found that when educators are not attending to the present moment, it is often because they are either "scattered by the moment" or "smothered by the moment." When they are scattered by the moment, they take their eye off the ball as a result of being pulled in too many different directions. They often complain of being "spread too thin." In a classroom, a scattered teacher may find herself teaching a lesson at the reading table, answering a question from a student who is not a member of the group, answering a call from the front office, and telling another child to not sharpen his pencil. Likewise, scattered leaders behave reactively, rather than proactively. They spend their days "putting out fires," moving from one meeting to the next, checking email, and responding to texts. We all encounter these very real challenges, but if we succumb to the scattered approach of attending, we will never be focused long enough to make the most of today so that it ensures a better tomorrow.

Conversely, when educators are "smothered by the moment," the opposite phenomenon occurs: They focus on the ball perhaps too intensely, not allowing themselves to take in what else is occurring around them. In the classroom, a smothered teacher may concentrate solely on delivering a lecture or presentation to the class and become so focused on what he is saying and doing and what he will say next, that he fails to notice subtle events occurring around the room that are adversely impacting his message. Smothered leaders may focus so single-mindedly on an important task that they stay in their offices for extended periods of time to make sure it gets done. While they're locked away behind closed doors, they miss the equally important events that are occurring throughout the school or district.

The best teachers and leaders encounter the same zany challenges faced by everyone in our profession. They too must keep up with a seemingly insurmountable number of duties and responsibilities. The difference is they never exhibit the scattered or smothered behaviors described above. Instead, in the "hash browns" school of attending to the present moment, they choose the "covered" approach. In this approach, classroom teachers and school administrators deftly attend to the present with an optimal balance of focusing on one thing without shutting out other important things occurring around them. They always keep in mind why they are doing what they are doing. They focus on their immediate goal and what is affecting it, and they demonstrate a keen ability to keep their eye on the goal without losing awareness of the bigger picture and what is impacting their path to the goal. Using a baseball analogy, despite all the people and challenges competing for their attention, they seem to have all the bases covered. They keep their eye on the ball, but also notice the positioning of the defensive players, the wind speed and direction, and the pitcher's tendencies. They are open to the stimuli around them, are able to respond appropriately to it, and have the presence of mind to apply the correct amount of attention to the central issue at hand while simultaneously monitoring peripheral ones. They have it all "covered," whether that means an unannounced safety drill, the inevitable technology glitch, or a lesson that does not go exactly as planned. They have a plan in place for each scenario and implement the plan with fierce intention. At the same time, they monitor their surroundings every step of the way and adjust accordingly to ensure future success.

When the three of us were together in Georgia recently, we immediately made our way to the nearest Waffle House. Todd ordered his hash browns scattered. Jimmy went with scattered, smothered, and chunked. Jeff opted for covered. When it comes to hash browns, we are supportive of each individual's personal preference. However, when attending to the present moment in order to achieve a better future for our schools, we strongly recommend only one option: covered!

Educators have so many opportunities to lose sight of the present moment—from looking ahead to upcoming events to obsessing about previous events or past performance. It is easy to take our eye off the ball: what is happening right now, in every classroom, in every school, in every cafeteria, hallway, playground, and with every student and staff member with whom we are interacting and serving. The most successful teachers and administrators we know have mastered the art of being present, focusing with a laser-like precision on the moment, whether they are teaching a lesson, having a conversation with a student or colleague, or holding a parent meeting. Of course, these great educators are also conscientious planners, who have looked ahead at the approaching units of instruction or professional learning opportunities. The lesson or event may be months or more down the road, but they are already thinking about what material they want to present and how it should be offered. Yet, while planning both short- and long-term events, they never lose sight of what is most important: the future that is unfolding before them, whether that is the child who needs their full attention or the colleague who stops by unexpectedly with a question. Good schools are made up of team members who never lose sight of today and the single lesson, the specific question, or the simple, kind gesture that may just make all the difference in the world to someone else down the road.

> ## The likelihood of a successful school year—for ourselves and our students—is based largely on the "small" victories we achieve today.

Being an educator is an awesome opportunity that is simultaneously, ridiculously challenging. When we are in the midst of a stressful school year, a myriad of responsibilities, tasks, duties, and events fly at us at head-spinning rates. Losing sight of the here and now to take care of what is coming next is always tempting as a strategy to save time; however, based on our experiences, the more we attend to what is before us this very moment and the less we try to multitask, look ahead, or dwell in the past, the more time we save in the long run. The better our collective focus is on this single day, the greater our chances of success for many tomorrows. The likelihood of a successful school year—for ourselves and our students—is based largely on the "small" victories we achieve today. Cumulatively, these small, daily victories will add up to a winning season. Excellent educators show the way to the future, in part, by attending to the present, regularly reminding others of where they are going, where they are now, and what the next immediate steps will be. They cherish every minute they have with the students they serve and do all they can today to equip them for success tomorrow. The best educators have a vision for the future, yet never forget to focus on every student, every day.

Communicate Early; Communicate Often

Educators who excel at *showing the way* to a common vision of the future also excel in the area of communication, a skill vital to classroom, school, and district success. Educators adept in the area of communication use a variety of formats for a variety of purposes. One important purpose is to show others a common vision of future hopes, dreams, and goals. Obviously, teachers cannot achieve the desired outcomes they seek from their students unless they first communicate precisely what it is they want students to know and be able to do. Not only must they clearly explain their expectations, they must also show students how to attain the desired outcome. In the same way, school leaders must communicate with teachers not only where they must go, but also how they will get there. Although they may not always realize it, teachers and school administrators are communicating almost every minute of every school day. The way they talk, listen, send emails, sit, stand, smile, laugh, use social media, and even the way they dress sends both explicit and implicit messages to the students, staff, and parents about who they are and what they stand for. Effective educators do not leave communication to chance, but instead build in specific methods for sharing their vision with others. They also do not settle for sharing this vision one time or in one way; instead, they share it early in the year and often thereafter, using a variety of tools in doing so. They know the why, what, and how of communication.

Why?

Sharing a vision is a central role of any educator—a vision paints a vivid picture of what things can be like for students, staff, and parents. It inspires people and helps to raise their hopes and expectations. When people are inspired, they are more likely to actively participate in the vision. Effective teachers and school administrators share their vision for their schools and classrooms regularly. Whenever you walk into the classroom or school of such educators, you see the vision boldly displayed both in words and in the behavior of the students and staff. Whenever you talk with these educators, you hear them describing what they are working towards. Whenever you read a written communication from these educators, you notice they are sending messages to remind others of their ultimate vision for the school, district, or classroom. These educators recognize the importance of talking about their vision whenever possible. They also know that the more they communicate it effectively to others, the more likely it is that they are creating a community of people who know about their vision and who will, potentially, be more likely to support it.

What?

Excellent teachers and leaders communicate a great deal of information. The information they communicate falls into six broad categories we like to call, "The 3 I's and the 3 C's":

- **Inform:** A primary purpose for communicating with students, staff, and parents is simply to provide information. Almost every communication delivered includes important information of some sort. One of the most important pieces of information they share with their communities is the vision they have for the work they are doing, whether they are teaching a class of kindergarten students or leading a school district of thousands of students and hundreds of teachers. At the outset of each school year, and frequently throughout the year, they inform those they serve about the "big picture."

- **Inspire:** Another purpose for communicating is to inspire others to share in the vision. Merely informing others about the vision will not guarantee they will be inspired by the vision. The best educators communicate in vivid ways to show why the vision matters and what benefits will be realized when it is achieved.

- **Include:** Excellent educators also communicate for the purpose of including others. They realize that not all parents, students, or staff respond in the same way, so they reach out in a variety of ways to ensure everyone is included. Through their communications, they also invite others to take part; rather than assuming students, staff, and parents will come along on the journey if they want to, these educators proactively reach out to create an inclusive environment.

- **Clarify:** Another purpose for communicating is to clarify what has been said before, perhaps saying it in a new way or sharing it in a new format. Excellent educators know that their message is not always received in the way it was intended, so they continue to reinforce it throughout the year.

- **Challenge:** Effective communicators also use their communications to challenge those they lead. Whether they are challenging their students to reach a new level of learning, parents to serve in their schools, or staff to go the extra mile on behalf of the school and its students, excellent educators are constantly communicating new challenges they hope others will accept in order to push the community toward achieving the common vision.

- **Celebrate:** A final and important purpose for communicating is to celebrate. High-performing educators know firsthand just how hard the work is and they value the effort others exert to help achieve a common vision. They take time to recognize individual and collective accomplishments, deeds, and results that are aligned with the stated vision. They never shy away from hard work themselves and are equally willing to enlist others in the work. At the same time, they never fail to recognize and celebrate many successes along the way.

HOW?

To be honest, the methods for communicating in today's society are so vast, that if you are not communicating in a variety of formats at this point, you are simply making a conscious decision not to do so. The best educators embrace and take advantage of the many new communication tools available. They employ an array of these tools, choosing ones designed to target all members of their audience. At the same time, they respect that some "old-fashioned" methods still do the job. Some of the most common and effective ways of communicating in schools include what Naisbitt, Naisbitt, and Phillips term both high tech and "high touch" methods.[3] Each of the following communication tools merits an entire book chapter itself, but, simply stated, here are the ten ways we see effective educators communicating most often in schools around the globe. The educators we know who are the most successful at communicating their vision do not rely on any single method, but employ all of these and more throughout a school year to keep the lines of communication open:

1. District/school/class websites

2. School mobile apps

3. Blogging

4. Podcasting

5. Notification and alert tools

6. Email

7. Social media (such as Twitter, Voxer, and Facebook)

8. Phone calls

9. Videos (such as a YouTube channel)

10. Handwritten notes

Excellent educators are also excellent communicators. One way they show others where they are going collectively and where individuals need to get to next is by communicating early and often with every member of their communities. They do not employ a one-size-fits-all communication strategy, but choose a variety of tools to communicate their vision and ensure that their communications are regular, two-way, and meaningful. To state that communication between and among all stakeholders in any organization is of paramount importance is to state the obvious. It's somewhat surprising, then, that survey results in far too many schools we visit decry "lack of communication" as a top problem. We must not take for granted that others know or share our sense of purpose and our future vision. Excellent teachers and leaders strategically plan and implement ongoing communications that *show the way* by informing, inspiring, including, clarifying, challenging, and celebrating.

Radio Station WIIFM

"When confronted with change, most people turn to their favorite radio station: WIIFM—What's In It For Me?"[4] This quote from a *Fast Company* by article Roger Dean Duncan was written for a business audience, but it applies to any career field—including education. People do care about how they are affected by change and how the organization's vision for the future impacts them. Of course, in education we are fortunate: Most students and staff members in our schools are not motivated exclusively by a financial bottom line or even job security and advancement. The vast majority of educators we know entered the profession for a simple and noble reason: They sincerely wanted to change lives for the better. Likewise, the vast majority of students willingly agree to do what their teachers ask of them. Still, when establishing a vision for the future, it behooves us to consider our students' and colleagues' concerns, questions, interests, hopes, and fears. Great classroom teachers and great school leaders make it a point to not only let others know where they are headed, but also how it will benefit them once they arrive. They create a vision for their students or colleagues with such clarity that it can be fully understood, and they explain the benefits in ways so compelling that others want to embrace the vision.

In discussing change, Winston Churchill wisely opined, "There is nothing wrong with change, if it is in the right direction." Establishing a vision for the future is to declare that we are willing to make changes over time to ensure we continue heading in the right direction—and that we ultimately arrive at our destination. The first important step in charting this course, obviously, is to ensure we have set our sights on the proper destination. In schools, the best way to guarantee that we have done so is to repeatedly ask the following question throughout the visioning process: "Is this what is best for kids?"

Doing what is best for kids is the "true north" for every excellent educator we know.

Doing what is best for kids is the "true north" for every excellent educator we know. Sure, they may make mistakes along the way, but they never lose sight of what, for them, is the true north path to student success. Once we have committed to doing what is best for the students we serve and have established a vision of what future success in this area will look like, we must then show the way forward to those we teach and lead. The finest teachers lay out a vision for the students they teach on an annual basis, letting each new group of students know what they will accomplish by the end of the school year. For excellent school leaders, these visions are likely longer-term propositions—a vision that is ongoing and revisited periodically to ensure the direction in which they are heading is still aligned to their true north. In both scenarios, the vision, on its surface, may well be appealing enough to almost all affected students and staff. However, in both scenarios, it is important to tell the truth: The vision will not be realized without a lot of hard work, dedication, and commitment. Although most students and staff support a noble vision, not all are willing to put forth the effort required to achieve it. Master teachers and leaders know this and, therefore, constantly tune in to radio station WIIFM, reminding the students or staff members they lead how the hard work will benefit them personally in the end.

Excellent educators address WIIFM artfully and confidently, rather than through power and authority. They focus less on negative consequences that may result from failure to realize the vision, and more on the wonder and possibilities that will exist when they do. Moreover, the wonders and possibilities on which they focus are intrinsic in nature, rather than extrinsic. Excellent reading teachers, for example, work to produce amazing readers. They do so because they want their students to develop a lifelong love of reading, not because they want their students to do well on a reading test. Let's be clear: They *do* want their students to perform well on the reading tests, but the test is not their *why,* or reason for teaching. The more they focus on instilling a lifelong love of reading and learning within their students, the more likely it is these students will perform well on standardized tests. Good test scores are rarely, if ever, the vision of excellent educators, but good test scores are often an associated secondary outcome of a more noble vision, such as producing students who love to read and learn.

The WIIFM cannot be satisfied through rewards and punishments. It is fulfilled when we authentically invest others in their own self-improvement. Although they may not always admit it, many students and staff wonder if they can even do what it is they are being asked to do and, at times, may wonder whether they even want to do what is being asked. Excellent teachers and school administrators behave intentionally to constantly make sure those they lead want to succeed and feel they can succeed.

Great educators are able to enlist students and staff in the collective vision for the future as well as each individual's role in achieving the vision. Their ability to enlist others in the vision coincides with their ability to motivate them. They know, however, that motivation comes primarily from within, not from someone else. Rather than motivating through a series of "carrots and sticks," they rely on the wisdom found in Daniel Pink's work on the topic, "driving" their students and colleagues on a journey to intrinsic motivation using Pink's formula of autonomy, mastery, and purpose as the vehicle.[5] Whenever we see students or staff truly motivated to accomplish a significant task, we also see teachers and leaders who have first and foremost connected the cause to something larger than any individual or any "bottom line." They connect the vision to core values, such as making a difference in the lives of kids, or even changing society for the better by molding better global citizens. They establish and regularly revisit the big picture *why* or, in Pink's model, *purpose*. Another common factor we notice in schools with noticeably motivated students and staff is a great deal of "voice and choice." The overall vision may be in place, and there are likely several non-negotiables associated with the overall vision, but students and staff are given autonomy—real control over various aspects of their work, whether that means deciding what to work on or when to do it. Likewise, they receive encouragement and meaningful feedback and the support they need to succeed along the paths they choose to take.

Students and teachers get better at what they do by engaging in ever-increasing, but attainable, challenging work.

A final common variable we notice in schools with motivated and invested students and staff members is related to what Pink calls "mastery." Students and teachers get better at what they do by engaging in ever-increasing, but attainable, challenging work. Motivating themselves, their colleagues, and their students to embrace the work on the road to mastery requires them to intentionally assign tasks and performances that push each individual just beyond their current level. They provide the students and staff they lead with what Pink calls "Goldilocks tasks," challenges that are neither overly difficult, nor overly simple. One source of frustration in classrooms and during professional learning sessions is the frequent mismatch between what people must do and what people can do. When what they must do exceeds their capabilities, the result is anxiety. When what they must do falls short of their capabilities, the result is boredom. The best educators work to find the sweet spot in between.

Some students and staff members at our schools have absolutely no vision of anything other than where they are right now. We can help our kids and fellow educators create a new and better vision for themselves through our words and actions. Excellent educators show others the way to a new and better future while also showing them why they would want to move in that direction by addressing the WIIFM question and motivating them to achieve it through the autonomy, mastery, and purpose formula of intrinsic motivation.

Sharing Our Stories

Excellent educators are masterful storytellers who never pass up a chance to share their stories as a way to show others endless possibilities. They also use storytelling to teach lessons, bring people together, express a vision for the future, promote empathy, and celebrate examples of people within the school or classroom making a difference. Stories can be a non-threatening way to share information with students and staff and a way to make the abstract concrete. Using social media to share stories about what is going on in their classrooms and schools can also be a great way for today's educators to build a brand for their district, school, or classroom. Storytelling can be a means for codifying the culture of a school or classroom. Excellent teachers and school leaders find and tell authentic stories that communicate their vision and purpose in ways that help others find their own meaning and sense of significance in the journey, empowering them, in turn, to share their own stories related to the quest. There is perhaps no more effective method of *showing the way* to future individual, classroom, and school success than by bringing it to life through stories that paint the picture of it happening in the past and present.

In the book *Made to Stick: Why Some Ideas Survive and Others Die*, brothers and coauthors Chip and Dan Heath outline six characteristics that increase the likelihood messages will be more readily retained by an audience.[6] In classrooms, of course, our primary audience includes every student in the class; our audience extends to staff when we are speaking to the entire school. It extends further still when we communicate with parents and our community members. It can even reach people around the globe when we share our stories with the world. Whether our audience is students, colleagues, parents, community members, or the entire world, if we can learn how to deliver messages in ways that "stick," audience members will be reminded time and again what we stand for, in what direction we are moving, and the progress we are making along the way. They will also be more likely to remain true to the collective vision of a better future.

The six qualities for successfully communicating ideas identified by the Heaths can be compacted into the acronym SUCCESs: Simple, Unexpected, Concrete, Credible, Emotional, and Story. Although the authors define each of these as separate entities that combine to create "sticky" ideas, the final one, Story, strikes us not only as the most powerful, but also one that is actually comprised of the other five. We compel others to act on our ideas when we engage them through effective storytelling. Effective stories include *concrete* and *credible* examples. They also contain *emotional* and *unexpected* events. Finally, they are often *simple* stories that can be clearly understood, remembered, retold, and acted upon. In the classroom, many master teachers disguise lectures as page-turning stories that our kids recall with clarity. Shrewd leaders share stories of school success as a way to promote what happened and increase the likelihood it will happen more often in the future. The authors believe in using three different types of stories for three different purposes:

1. Challenge Stories (to overcome obstacles)

2. Connection Stories (to get along or reconnect)

3. Creativity Stories (to inspire a new way of thinking)

Excellent educators use all three as a way to challenge, connect, and inspire the students and staff members they serve.

In a great teacher's classroom, the teacher is only one of many storytellers in the room. The students in these classrooms are empowered to be storytellers, also. Moreover, the teacher is no longer the student's sole audience. The most effective teachers take advantage of today's new and better communication tools, extending student voice well beyond the four walls of the classroom. In a similar fashion, savvy school administrators are no longer the sole storytellers of what occurs in their schools. They empower teachers, parents, students, and others to show and share what is happening in their schools through blog posts, Tweets, podcasts, Skype sessions, and a host of other communication platforms. Teachers know that students are more likely to put forth their best effort when they have a legitimate voice and an authentic audience. The same holds true for us as educators; if we truly believe in what we are doing and we have the opportunity to share what we are doing with the world, we are much more likely to put forth our very best effort each and every day.

Students are more likely to put forth their best effort when they have a legitimate voice and an authentic audience. The same holds true for us as educators.

Many of the excellent teachers and school administrators we know describe their role not as a "job," but as a "calling." We are reminded of a story that a pastor included in the weekly bulletin at her church. It was titled "Pushing Against the Rock." Without going into all the biblical references, it was simply about a man who was commanded to continuously push against a large rock, which he did for many years with no immediately discernible results. After many years of apparent failure, the frustrated man questioned what he was doing wrong and why he had failed. The answer given to him was that he had not failed at all; his calling was to be obedient and faithful and he had exhibited trust in following through on this calling. In the end, he had developed a strong back, arms, and legs through his daily efforts, and the rock was moved for him as a reward for his faithful efforts. Like the man in the story, great educators may not immediately see the rewards of their daily toil. Although the difference may be imperceptible in the present moment, they and the students they serve are growing stronger each and every day. Knowing that people can become frustrated when they do not see immediate results, excellent educators constantly share success stories—and encourage others to do the same—throughout the journey as a way to keep hope alive and keep everyone pushing against the rock in the right direction, with a purpose, and with the assurance that it will all be worthwhile.

Create, Don't Critique

No matter how grand the vision, or how effective the educator sharing the vision, pushback—from students in our classrooms and colleagues in our schools—is inevitable. Excellent educators are no different from anyone else in this regard. Even the best among us must respond to the classroom or school CYBO: *Chief "Yeah, But" Officer.* The difference between amazing educators and average ones lies in their response to criticism, reluctance, resistance, or indifference. They avoid the temptation to criticize in return and, instead, focus on creating. The students and staff in our schools who are most negative and least engaged in the vision of the future do not need more negativity or criticism; rather, they need a reason to join the movement. Excellent teachers and excellent leaders make sure to share those reasons.

The most important "thing" they create is not a thing at all, but an almost palpable feeling: They create joy. It may sound corny, but the best teachers and leaders are joyful people in general and, even when they are not in a joyful mood, never let others know. They exude an ongoing, ever-present attitude of joy whenever they are around the students they teach or the staff members they lead. When we ask students to describe inspiring teachers (or teachers to describe their most inspiring leaders), inevitably we hear them use words like, "energy," "optimism," "hope," "enthusiasm," and "fun." They are described as passionate, humorous, smiling people who have a bounce in their step and are always encouraging others to do their best. Obviously, it takes no special intellect or advanced degree to spread joy, neither does it happen by accident. Amazing educators are amazing humans who experience all human emotions at times, including sadness, frustration, and self-doubt. The difference is that they forge ahead regardless, not letting their own bad days transfer to those with whom they interact. Excellent educators create joyful learning environments and behave joyfully—even when they are not particularly joyful.

Another important "thing" excellent educators try to instill in others and throughout their classrooms and schools is a culture of curiosity. In *The World is Flat*, author Thomas L. Friedman claims that no one works harder than a curious kid and suggested that these words should be emblazoned above the doors of school entrances.[7] We agree and also believe that adults who are curious work harder as well. When amazing teachers are faced with the inevitable comment, "This is boring," or when an amazing administrator hears a teacher say, "But we have always done it this way," they refrain from criticizing. Instead, they seize the moment as opportunity to create curiosity within the person who is complaining. One of our favorite stories about the power of creating curiosity comes from a sixth-grade teacher in Fall Creek, Wisconsin. On the last day of school before high-school graduation, a group of graduating seniors were seen sprinting to their former sixth-grade teacher's classroom. This middle-school teacher, on these students' first day of sixth grade nearly seven years earlier, brought out a black box of some kind, talked about it, described it, discussed what might be inside it, and then said to them: "If you want to know what's in the box, come back and see me on your last week here before your high-school graduation." And that was it. That's all he ever mentioned about it. He never said another word about the black box, did not remind them about it, nothing. Just before graduation, they all just ran down there, joyfully demanding to know what was in the box! This teacher knew what all great educators know: Creating curiosity within others can have a powerful and long-lasting effect. (As an aside, when others asked the kids what was in the box, they refused to reveal the secret!)

Creating curiosity within others can have a powerful and long-lasting effect.

A final way excellent educators *create* when others might choose to *critique* is by creating opportunities to dream. Rather than criticize a student who shows no strong desire to learn or demonstrates very little interest in the subjects they are learning, great teachers create ways to awaken dreams within them. When great school leaders are faced with teachers who rarely volunteer to go the extra mile by leading a committee, sponsoring a student club, or attending a school event, their first response is not to criticize, but to create ways to engage these reluctant staff members. These teachers and leaders know that all students and staff members have dreams of their own and visions of greatness within them, even the ones who show no outward signs of having any such aspirations. We worked with one school principal who kicked off the start of one school year with the theme, "Making Dreams Come True," and suggesting that schools—much like Disney—are in the dream business. This principal emphasized at the outset of the year that all the students in the school had dreams for their future, and that it was their job to first learn what each individual's dream was, and then to create opportunities for helping them achieve their dreams for the year. She modeled this by asking each staff member to share—publicly or privately—what their own dream was for the upcoming school year. The response was so powerful, that she could barely keep up with all the new initiatives staff members wanted to start. She instituted a process for responding to new requests with a simple dream-come-true mantra: "Dream a dream, find a team, one-page paper." Whenever a staff member—or student—had a new idea they wanted to see happen at the school, the principal—or teacher—would encourage the dreamer, with the only requirement being that they find at least one other person to help make the dream happen and write a brief description of the dream, including why they wanted it to happen and what it would entail. This principal, along with an inspired staff, awakened the dreams of many within the school, including some who they had previously nearly written off.

Serving as an educator is rewarding. It is also a very demanding and exhausting endeavor. Even our most tireless and effective colleagues are sometimes met with negativity when sharing their vision and attempting to enlist others in their vision. When faced with negativity, though, they avoid responding in kind and treat these as opportunities to create joy, curiosity, and dreams.

Basic Instinct

No, this has nothing to do with the racy 1992 film of that title! Instead, we use it to refer to an interesting characteristic of many excellent educators we know: their tendency to go with their gut intuition, trusting in what they feel instinctively compelled to do when leading a group of teachers or students. Although excellent educators seem to possess a near-perfect, 20/20 vision of where they want to go, when pressed to describe where these visions come from, many of these amazing educators profess relative ignorance, suggesting something along the lines of, "I'm not sure; it just seemed like the right thing to do." Although they may not be able to immediately explain the source of their own inspiration and vision for those they served, each of these teachers and leaders with whom we spoke indicated they often trusted their instincts, or what one superintendent called his "internal compass" when deciding where they were headed and how they would show others the way forward.

> **Master educators are not afraid to leverage their natural intuition.**

Many of the behaviors we have written about in this section—attending to the present, communicating regularly, sharing stories, and creating joy—are behaviors that many excellent educators do instinctively. We suspect that all educators, in fact, have a similar instinctual sense of what to do; the truly excellent ones among us are simply more willing to act on their instincts without waiting for data, research, or pilot programs to prove their gut feeling correct. We can think of scores of successful teachers and leaders who have been described as having great instincts and people who follow their hunches. We can think of hundreds more who likely possess these same instincts and hunches, but are much less likely to act on them. Master educators are not afraid to leverage their natural intuition as a way to help them make better decisions about any number of mini-crises they face each day, from how to deal with a classroom-management problem, to how best to defuse a heated parent meeting, to whether they should call on social service agencies to intervene in a family situation. Such decisions are all important; many are urgent. When they are both important and urgent, excellent educators do not waver or wait. They act. Because they "know their stuff," they may have some learned knowledge that supports their decision, but even without scientific evidence, they are willing to act solely on instinct.

Several years ago, when Jeff was serving as a principal, he encouraged a sharp young assistant principal to apply for principal positions within the district. The assistant principal replied that he was not yet ready. When Jeff asked why, the response was, "I don't have the vision thing yet. When you came on board as principal, you really had a vision for where you wanted the school to go." Jeff's response was a somewhat incredulous: "I did?" Being known as a visionary administrator or leader is nice, but it may not be as strategic a move as some might think. It often starts simply by being passionate about some aspect of the work and then following that passion persistently, while relying on your internal compass to guide you about the next steps along the path to your ultimate destination.

In an ongoing era of high-stakes testing and holding all educators accountable for the results they produce, we have become accustomed to basing decisions on scads of data. In such environments, it can be intimidating to take action by simply following that little voice inside us, making a recommendation that may be met with resistance and, worse yet, might prove to be wrong. Too often, however, we see the opposite occurring—teachers and administrators backing off their first instinct, deciding not speak up or take action on something they feel strongly about based on intuition. More often than not, these same people later regret not acting upon their hunches when the path taken proves less successful than the outcomes the road not taken might have produced. Educators have hundreds of opportunities every day to speak up, suggest action steps, intervene in delicate situations, ask for what they want, propose new ideas, and pose provocative questions. Our challenge to excellent educators everywhere is to go for it: When in doubt, don't be afraid to trust your basic instincts!

TEACH 4, LEAD 4, LEARN 4

Teachers and leaders with whom we have worked and who stand out as truly excellent exhibit a clear pattern of *showing the way* in all that they do. They know what their vision is, both as individual educators and as part of a larger school community. Rather than try to *sell* this vision to the students they teach or the adults they lead, they *inspire* others to share in the vision, involving others every step of the way and inviting them to join in the journey. They begin by forming a vision in their own minds of what a better tomorrow looks like. They support innovation and innovators in their schools and classrooms, so that thinking and doing in new and better ways becomes ingrained in the culture. They keep an eye out for what's ahead without losing sight of what is happening in the moment. They make the most of today so that they are better equipped for tomorrow. They communicate regularly and in a variety of ways to remind others of the vision and celebrate small wins as they occur. They know the importance of letting those they teach and lead know how changes along the way will benefit them specifically. They share stories frequently, showing examples of the vision in action. They create classroom and school cultures marked by joy, curiosity, and making dreams come true. Finally, although they are well versed in best practices and current research and are mindful of all available data relating to student and staff performance, they are not afraid to trust their instincts when making important decisions.

Teach 4

Here are four educators who we believe stand out as exemplars for *Showing the Way*:

1. Kara Welty (@kara_welty) is a mentor teacher and a technology integrationist leading 1:1 learning at a model school in the Kansas City area. Kara also taught both first and sixth grade for years and is widely respected for her ability to connect with students of all backgrounds. Whether working with students or staff, Kara chooses to *create, not critique* when enlisting others to share in her vision.

> *As an educator who has taught both first and sixth grade, I have found that creating a vision in my classroom is the foundation of a positive culture that will thrive throughout the year. This ideology has proved itself effective time and time again while working with students who possess a myriad of behaviors and needs. Through these meaningful experiences, I have realized how building a strong community is not just crucial on the first day of school; it is vital for every minute of every school day. Furthermore, I have seen the highest levels of success with this process when students and I create a shared vision together. Otherwise, if I create a vision without their valuable input, it will not be "OUR" vision; it will just be "MY" vision. When students feel empowered to make decisions, their trust blossoms. But I must add that creating a vision is not enough. The vision students and I create together is continually resurfaced, practiced, and communicated through our words, actions, and attitudes. Throughout the year, if I notice resistance or withdrawal from a student, I take a moment to reflect upon the growing issue before I jump to conclusions or frustrations. Instead of leading with critique, I make a conscientious effort to talk genuinely to that student. Through these heartfelt observations and conversations, I ask students questions like, "What can I do to help you?" and "What do*

you need to be successful next time?" Each time I show students that their voice matters and that we are on the same team, I see relationships grow right before my eyes. Ultimately, as we continue moving toward our class or school vision, I am reminded that persistence and compassion will be our trusted companions. The journey to growth may be difficult, but when we make our future vision the priority, students will win every single time.

2.   Aric Foster (@Aricfoster2) is a high-school English teacher in Armada, Michigan. He is also a contributing author of *Hacking Assessment*, an adjunct professor at Concordia University, and a student intern liaison at Oakland University. As a classroom teacher, Aric is charged with teaching a large number of students a large number of standards by the end of each course he teaches. To help him accomplish all that he must in order to realize his ultimate destination, he maintains a *future focus while attending to the present.*

Perhaps the most common and obvious way teachers attend to the present while also focusing on the future is through the proper use of pre- and post-tests. As in many classrooms, in my room, learners take a pre-test during the first week of school and a similar test during the last week of school. While the most obvious focus of this practice is the future (Can learners improve over our time together?), it certainly attends to the present. Early in my teaching career, I only treated this pre/post process as data collection to report to administration for teacher-evaluation purposes. It was only during the past seven years that I used pre-test data to influence my teaching. For example, at the beginning of the 2015-2016 school year, I noticed that my English 11 juniors performed poorly on the questions that addressed "identifying author's craft." I initially planned on giving this topic only cursory attention later in the year, as I assumed this was a topic in which most learners were proficient before entering my room. However, upon careful contemplation of this data, I added "analyzing author's craft" as a prominent stan-dard in my standards-based learning classroom during the first unit of the year. I then altered previously planned formative tasks, and added new ones, to address this gap. Finally, I included this topic on the first summative assessment. While I did see growth from pre-test performance to summative assessment performance, I revisited this standard periodically throughout the year. As a result, my learners performed well on this section of the post-test at the end of the school year.

3. Megan Moran (@MeganCMoMo) is a high-school math teacher in suburban Schaumburg, Illinois. Megan has stepped out of traditional teaching in both methods and philosophy. Taking risks and trusting her *basic instinct*, she takes pride in sharing her experiences with other educators in hopes that they, too, will push themselves and their students.

I was the typical teacher in my eighth year. I lectured, did group work, gave assignments out of the textbook, gave quizzes, graded, reviewed, and gave tests. My classroom was no different than the many classrooms in which I was a student a decade prior and, other than my confidence, not much had changed in my classroom since I started teaching—well, except the students. Some may argue that students today are the same, but I will kindly disagree and say that students today require more engaging classroom activities to learn. I knew I needed to change because my students were not learning, and they lacked the confidence to persevere independently.

After some reflection on the broken learning cycle in my classroom, I took a leap of faith and trusted my gut to make a big change—a change my school had not yet seen. I created video lessons, reworked in-class practice, and completely "flipped" my classroom. This was two years before my district went one-to-one, which, honestly, I knew nothing about. I just knew that I had to reach my students in a different way. I wanted them to take ownership in their learning, build confidence, and increase their understanding of the concepts to prepare them for the next course in mathematics. The results surprised even me. Students watched my video lessons as many times as they needed, tried to "pause and rewind me" on days I gave direct instruction, and their retention and comprehension often exceeded that of my colleagues' students.

I had little idea how well flipping my curriculum would work, or that I would end up flipping three courses over the next five years. I trusted my instinct to do something different and sought experts in the area. I connected with other "flippers," attended conferences, and eventually started giving presentations and trainings on flipped classrooms. Teachers act with instinct every day we interact with students—sometimes in conversation, sometimes in action. For me, tapping into my innate teacher gut and then pursuing research and support to make a major change in my instruction made the most impact on student learning.

4. **Laura Fleming (@LFlemingEDU)** is a library media specialist in New Milford, New Jersey. She is also the author of the bestselling book, *Worlds of Making*. Although Laura is a natural innovator who is recognized around the world for the innovative advances she has made, she views herself not so much as an innovator, but as someone who *supports innovation* among the school communities she serves.

My career as an educator began as a classroom teacher. After several years, I transitioned to the role of a school library media specialist. In this role, I felt that I could take liberties outside of the traditional classroom cannon that classroom teachers were not able to. I drew upon the depth of knowledge about instructional technology that I had gained as a classroom teacher and applied it in more innovative applications. I became passionate about using current research and cutting-edge technology to discover creative ways to assist educators in reaching learning goals and was able to work with colleagues in applying innovative methods and new technology into their fields of expertise.

The vision I have for our library directly relates to the mission of our district: providing engaging, participatory, authentic, learner-centered, innovative learning experiences and opportunities for both students and staff. Our school, with the library as its hub, will equip each student with the necessary tools they will need to lead productive lives in today's ever-changing society. To support this vision, I collaborate with classroom teachers to design, implement, and evaluate highly innovative lessons that provide learning opportunities for all abilities and interests, while at the same time meeting curricular requirements and integrating twenty-first-century technology tools.

My long-term commitment is to continue to design an excellent school library program that boosts student achievement and to support and challenge instruction that recognizes and facilitates innovation. As an early adopter of new technology, I support others in our learning community to continually implement best practices and new technologies. I keep a pulse on what future technology will bring. Some students and teachers seek me out for support; in other instances, when I know certain teachers or students may be hesitant to reach out, I seek them out and invite them to partner with me on an innovative project I think they might enjoy trying. I feel it is part of my job to show them how anyone can become an innovator and why it matters. Not everyone in our school is at the same point along the "innovation continuum," and that is absolutely OK. My role in supporting others is simply to make sure everyone feels comfortable moving forward from where they currently are, wherever that may be.

Lead 4

Here are four educators who currently serve in formal educational leadership roles who we believe stand out as exemplars for *Showing the Way*:

1. **Glenn Robbins (@Glennr1809)** is superintendent of Tabernacle Township School District in New Jersey. Prior to this role, Glenn served as a middle-school principal in New Jersey and was recognized as a 2016 NASSP Digital Principal of the Year. As a principal, Glenn implemented significant changes in the school schedule, school learning spaces, and teaching and learning practices. When he established an audacious vision of change for his school, Glenn knew his teachers would likely support the vision, but he also knew he would have to address the question, "*WIIFM?*"

"What is the experience we are trying to create?" This is the question I asked prior to establishing our vision for the future of our school when I was a principal. I believe all leaders should be asking this when creating a new vision for their school or district. School leaders have a responsibility to create and nourish the kind of work environment people always envisioned when they decided to become educators. We need to focus on relationships, optimism, and revamping current school systems into places that promote curiosity, wonder, and awe, for not only students, but also staff. Change in education has been a constant, and to successfully affect wide-scale change initiatives, we must earn the trust and belief of our colleagues. While leaders are mandated with reforms, it's the transparency and trust that one shows in working alongside his staff— instead of simply giving directives—that builds culture and climate.

When establishing a vision for the future that will require staff members to change their current reality, I find it important to openly let them know what the changes will require of them. I also attempt to show them how—in the long run—it will benefit them, even though the work ahead may be challenging. One way I try to inspire support for the vision is by actively inviting staff and students to design, iterate, and act upon the vision in pursuit of reaching their ultimate goals—which, for educators, tend to be all about bettering the lives of others. We need to empower staff members to become passionate leaders who guide our vision of creating a learning environment where everyone is excited about the work we are doing. Educators, by and large, don't enter this profession for personal gain, but they do have personal needs we must consider. For many, that need is to ensure that any changes we make will be better for the kids they serve; "What's In It For Them?" tends to be more along the lines of, "Will this help me better serve the kids?" If the answer is "yes," I have found most educators willing to join the effort. As leaders, we owe it to all educators to reawaken their inner fire to make the lives of others better.

2. Tony Sinanis (@TonySinanis) is currently a lead learner at Plainedge Schools on Long Island in New York. Tony received the 2014 New York State Elementary Principal of the Year Award and the national 2013 Bammy Award for Elementary School Principal of the Year. Tony is the coauthor of *Telling Your School's Story*. As a school leader for many years and now a central office leader, Tony knows the importance of *sharing our stories*, both as a way to show the community what is happening in our schools and to promote the vision among those teaching, learning, and leading within the schools.

As a long-time school leader and current district leader, I keep coming back to three words: relationships, culture, and vision. As I gained more experience as a leader and spent more time listening to those around me, I came to understand how interconnected those concepts are and that a shift in one will influence the others. In fact, based on my experiences, it was clear that healthy relationships (or unhealthy relationships, depending on the context) shaped the culture of a school, which influenced the vision. Relationships and culture, which are mainly internal characteristics of an educational organization, are the crux of the vision. In turn, the vision becomes the external representation of the culture of a space; the vision becomes the "brand" of a school; and the vision becomes the table of contents or epilogue of a school or district story.

During my time at Cantiague (2008–2016), I wasn't quite sure about the best way to capture and represent our vision statement, especially in thinking about the fact that we had dedicated ourselves to focusing on twenty-first-century skills both in our teaching and learning. Although twenty-first-century skills emphasize critical thinking and collaboration, we also wanted to find a way to celebrate and recognize our dedicated efforts to meaningfully integrate technology into the teaching and learning experiences each day at Cantiague.

After a month of discussion on this topic with a team of students, parents, and staff, we kept coming back to the idea of a video and how it might best capture the Cantiague experience and would allow us to actually **show**, with images, what the vision statement looks like in school. We wanted to bring our vision statement to life because we felt that energy would capture the true essence of our school. We wanted to focus on our kids and all the various facets of their experiences as learners in our space. We wanted to spotlight everything that was amazing about our school, because there were awesome things happening every single day. The video we created was a visual representation of our vision statement—one we could share in our school and with the members of our community. It is the introduction to our collective story, and it beautifully shows the relationships and culture of our community.

3. Rosa Perez-Isiah (@rosaisiah) is a principal at an elementary school in California. She leads with passion, purpose, and a social justice lens. As principal, Rosa knows the importance of creating a vision shared by all within the school community. She also knows that if the entire community is going to have clarity about the vision and commit to the vision, she—as the primary leader of the school—must start the process herself by having *20/20 vision* about her own hopes and dreams for the students, staff, and parents she serves.

Every school and school district needs a vision statement. Typically, these are captivating statements about the organization's beliefs and commitment to the skillful work necessary for transformational change. Unfortunately, in my experience, the vision is often lost in the day-to-day management of the organization. Well-intentioned people become consumed by the work of who we are instead of the visionary work of who we want to be. Where does the vision begin, how do we maintain focus, and most importantly, who is responsible for moving that vision from a slogan to a living, breathing reality? The work of moving our schools from vision to reality begins with the leader. A leader with a strong and clear vision has the power to motivate the masses, challenge comfort zones, and inspire change. A great leader understands her primary role in the organization as a communicator of the vision and someone who models the change. She creates a committed following by inspiring and motivating the team toward the vision. The ability to meet the needs of an organization while envisioning and executing change is the primary responsibility of the leader. The envisioning process calls for courageous and action-oriented leaders who trust, are trusted, and who possess a passion for this great work. True leadership is the capacity to translate a vision statement into a shared reality, lived out by all within the organization. It requires intentional focus and must begin with a visionary leader.

4. Becky Ince (@PrincipalInce) is a principal at Central Monmouth Intermediate School in Monmouth, Illinois. As a school administrator, Becky knows the importance of communicating clearly with students, staff, parents, and the entire school community. To help her keep all stakeholders focused on the path ahead, Becky *communicates early and communicates often* in a variety of ways.

Every successful organization, whether it is in the world of business, athletics, industry, or politics, has effective communication practices in place. In the field of education, with stakeholders that are many and varied, communication is essential in establishing the leader's purpose and vision, as well as bringing into focus what the leader deems important. To make a school vision a reality and to ensure we connect with all stakeholders, I err on the side of over-communicating our vision using a variety of tools. Since becoming the principal at a grade school in west central Illinois, I recognized the need to create efficient channels of communication for members of my staff, district faculty, families, the community, and the businesses in our district. To communicate our vision to my staff, I publish a weekly electronic memo using Weebly as the host. This memo shares basic reminders, provides links for teachers that support best teaching practices, spotlights student and teacher accomplishments from the classroom, and includes a section where I express my thoughts, our vision, and—at times—my concerns with what is taking place in the building. Through Twitter and Facebook, we communicate with pictures and words to share the successes in our building and post reminders about important events. Social media allows us to tell our school story in a positive way. In the words of Rollo May, "Communication leads to community, that is, to understanding, intimacy, and mutual valuing."

Learn 4

Here are four resources/tools/action steps you can use to further develop yourself and others relating to the standard we call *Showing the Way*:

1. Watch this short video from RapidStart Leadership: How to Write an Inspiring Vision Statement.[8] In this video, Ken Downer shares specific tips for crafting a vision statement that is clear, simple, aspirational, visual, and future focused. Learn the characteristics of a good vision statement and what to do with it once you have one.

How to Write an
Inspiring Vision
Statement

2. Read "Teaching That Sticks,"[9] an article written by Chip Heath and Dan Heath, the authors of the book *Made to Stick: Why Some Ideas Survive and Others Die*. In this short article, the Heaths apply their six principles of "stickiness" to learning in schools.

Teaching That Sticks

3. Create a school or classroom vision statement. A school or classroom vision statement should reflect the long-term aspirations and goals for the school or classroom, the future hopes and dreams of those working within. The vision statement should be brief and easy to remember, spelling out what you ultimately envision for your school or classroom. The vision should be recognized by all staff or students as an indication of where they are headed. The vision statement communicates to everyone involved where they are headed and inspires them to become better. Your vision is all about the future you want to create for the community you wish to impact.

The following steps to take when crafting your school or classroom vision statement are adapted from the book, *Learning by Doing*:[10]

1. Describe the school (or classroom) you are trying to create.

2. Describe what the school (or classroom) would look like if it were a great place for students. What would it look like if it were a great place for teachers?

3. It is five years from now (or the end of the year for a classroom vision) and you have achieved your vision as a school (or classroom). Describe how you are different, including what is going on in terms of results, relationships, practices, and climate.

4. Imagine you have been given sixty seconds on the nightly news to clarify the vision of your school (or classroom) to the local community. Write a script for what you would want to say.

Check out 30 Example Vision Statements.[11] In addition to the statements themselves, they provide five key findings about the best vision statements that are quite interesting.

30 Example Vision Statements

4. Watch this whiteboard animation video, Dan Pink – Autonomy, Mastery, and Purpose.[12] This short animation shows Pink's three motivational factors that lead to better performance and personal satisfaction.

Dan Pink – Autonomy, Mastery, and Purpose

GO THE WAY

Followers do what a leader does long before they do what a leader says. Leaders must model the desired behavior.
—Steve Keating

Take a moment to think about someone in your life who you consider a leader. What stands out about them more in your memory, the words they said or the actions they performed? Although we suspect you can recall examples of both, we also suspect that—as is so often the case—their actions spoke louder than their words. Excellent teachers and leaders go the way they want others to follow. They know that actions speak louder than words and realize that students and staff may listen to what they say, but definitely observe what they do. As a result, they are acutely aware of both the words they speak and the actions they take, intentionally setting the example they wish to see in and from others. Our very best teachers and leaders have extremely high expectations for the students and teachers they serve— and even higher expectations for themselves. They would not ask others to go where they are not willing to go themselves. Great teachers and leaders are master "modelers," who demonstrate for others what they expect in terms of the all-important ABCs: the attitudes, behaviors, and commitments necessary for long-term success. They are "doers" who are not afraid to work alongside others as they go the way for excellence.

DEFINING THE STANDARD: GOING THE WAY FOR EXCELLENCE

The third standard of teaching and leading for excellence exhibited by dedicated, focused, and relentless educators with whom we have worked is all about "walking the talk"—performing actions consistent with one's claims and aligned with group norms and an established common mission and vision. As with the preceding two standards, we have provided details and indicators to watch for below and offer this brief definition for what it means to *Go the Way*: **Serving as a model for others through daily communications, actions, and values "lived out loud," in order to establish deeply embedded "ways of being" that contribute to an overall culture of integrity, respect, encouragement, and dedication.**

STANDARD OF EXCELLENCE #3
Excellent Teachers and Leaders Go the Way

Excellent teachers and leaders consistently model for others in their districts, schools, departments, and classrooms how to learn, listen, and lead. They teach and lead by doing and "being," demonstrating for others best practices in teaching, learning, and leading.

INDICATORS

- Develops cooperative relationships among the people with whom they work

- Actively listens to diverse points of view

- Treats others with dignity and respect daily

- Supports decisions that people make on their own

- Cultivates trusting relationships with students, staff, and parents

- Gives people a great deal of choice and freedom in deciding how to do their work

- Models for others what they expect of them

- Follows through on the promises and commitments they make

- Is present, visible, and accessible

- Sets clear and lofty standards for self and others

- Embraces diversity and dissent

- Encourages and elicits open and honest debate

- **Focuses on the question, "How must we behave on a daily basis in order to fulfill our vision and achieve our mission?" and models desired behaviors consistently.**

Why It Matters

Excellent educators begin their preparation for success by acquiring the necessary knowledge and skills; next they show others how they, too, can acquire new knowledge and skills and how the classroom, school, or district overall can collectively reach new heights if everyone is committed to ongoing growth and self-improvement. However, even if everyone on the team is highly qualified, competent, and committed to ongoing personal and professional growth, the quest for collective excellence will fall apart if the leader (or teacher) does not consistently say and do the things he or she said were important to say and do. Moreover, the leader (or teacher) must be highly transparent, allowing everyone in the classroom, department, school, or district to see that their words and actions are in alignment. In other words, they must model the agreed-upon values. Educators who go the way in this manner are people who treat others with dignity and respect ten days out of ten and expect others to do the same. Having said that, they are not perfect and, at times, may fall short of their own expectations. When they do, they again go the way they would want others to go by acknowledging their mistake, offering a sincere apology, and not making the same mistake again. They are professionals who are often described as people of integrity and who are trusted by students and staff who know them.

People are always watching to see if we really mean what we say.

One of the greatest things about being an educator is that it matters so darn much. What is challenging about serving as an educator is that it matters each and every second of each and every day that we are in our classrooms and schools. People are always watching to see if we really mean what we say, whether it is a student in a classroom who wonders if his teacher really means it when she gives a direction or a staff member who wonders if the principal really means it when he says something is a "non-negotiable." The answer in either situation can almost always be found in the actions teachers and leaders take: Are they doing what they said they would do? Are they doing themselves what they are asking others to do? Are they consistent, fair, and respectful to all? Do they want open and honest debate in their classrooms and schools and invite diverse points of view? If the answer to these questions is a resounding, "yes," it affirms for others that the work they are doing and the vision they are striving for is important.

When we consistently align our actions with our words, it validates for our very best people that what they are doing is right. It also makes clear to our mediocre performers that "mediocre" is not good enough and that they, too, will need to improve.

The most outstanding teachers and leaders we know continue their journey on the path to excellence by living out their professional and personal lives based on deeply held core values. Even if they have never publicly shared these values with their students or colleagues, if asked, we suspect that those who know them would be able to accurately describe such values. These educators move beyond simply having—and acting upon—such values for themselves; in addition, they work to establish commonly held values among the students and fellow educators with whom they work. They create classroom, school, and district cultures in which all members know what is important, what is expected, and what things must never occur. They encourage others to invest in these values and hold themselves and others accountable when they stray from these. Excellent teachers and leaders know that perhaps nothing will sabotage their efforts for a brighter tomorrow more quickly than acting contrary to the ways they said they would act. With that understanding, they identify, share, and adhere to their deeply held values. They not only know the way to success themselves and show others the way to success; they also go the way along the path to success, moving consistently and reliably in that forward direction, each and every day.

What It Looks Like

Be That One Moment

Effective teachers and leaders never stop modeling positive interactions. They recognize that every interaction with a student, parent, or staff member is one single moment to inspire more positive interactions and to impact every person they encounter in a positive way. Imagine a school where students and adults all modeled this one simple act at every opportunity, where *everyone* brought their best one moment to every introduction, encounter, greeting, or gesture. No day in school is free of challenges. The never-ending stream of problems that flows across our classroom and office desks can leave even the most positive and passionate educators feeling exhausted and depleted. It is easy to get sucked into the minutiae of the daily grind and fall into the trap of dealing with trivial things that drain our energy and overfill our cup. Regardless, teachers and leaders who go for excellence stay focused and manage the daily interruptions and challenges by providing themselves with a little bit of reprieve by keeping themselves refreshed and energized. They begin by recognizing and accepting their own circumstances, emptying their cup of the daily messes they find, reshifting their attitudes, and then dedicating their time and energy to filling the cup of those they serve.

One evening, Jimmy and Jeff were attending a *What Great Educators Do Differently* conference and having dinner with one of the principal attendees who began to share his frustrations about what he felt was a lack of support from his superintendent. He went on to explain how he had been excited about the potential of creating a new program at his school and had invested several days and evenings working with his staff to devise a plan that they felt confident would make a strong impact on their school community. He noted that he had scheduled a meeting with his superintendent and was excited to tell him about the plan. Barely thirty seconds into that meeting, the superintendent interrupted him, sharing his apprehension about the potential costs and other logistical concerns he had about the program. As the principal tried to explain that he and his team had taken those concerns into account and had come up with possible solutions, the superintendent once again cut him off mid-sentence and then hijacked the conversation, bombarding him with questions. As the superintendent's concerns piled up, it became clear to the principal that the plan was already dead. Understandably, the principal left that meeting not only frustrated, but devastated and feeling like a failure.

Throughout our careers, we have heard dozens of similar stories from students, teachers, and leaders having the "lid put on them" by others who could not see beyond their own perspectives to the visions and dreams of others who wanted to achieve something beyond the status quo—to go for greatness! We are here to tell you that there is nothing more demoralizing than watching others put themselves on the line in an effort to do something extraordinary for their students, staff, or community, only to be left feeling completely defeated. The good news is that this feeling is never experienced by those in classrooms, schools, or districts that are led by exceptional educators. On the contrary, those students and teachers leave the classroom or meeting even more excited than when they went in to share their ideas. Excellent teachers and excellent leaders know how to move others in a way that motivates them to learn more, do more, and be more than they ever imagined possible. In other words, they not only know how to fill their own cups, but they also know and model for others how to refill their own cups—as well as the cups of their students, staff, and parents. They go out of their way to inspire others to aspire for excellence.

Excellent educators realize that by keeping things in perspective and filling the cups of others, so too, then, are their own cups filled. Talented educators look beyond their immediate situation and are able to approach their work by thinking about how they conduct themselves moment by moment. One practical way to ensure we bring our best to every experience is to bring a positive attitude to every situation we encounter, regardless of the severity of the situation. We can never forget that our bodies are listening to everything our minds think and our mouths speak. So if our mindset is projecting an attitude of "we shall overcome," then our body language and our actions will mirror the same beliefs which, in turn, leads to the types of behaviors we want to emulate in our hallways, classrooms, cafeterias, and office areas. Simply put, we become what we believe. Excellent educators consistently model positivity in all that they do, especially when encouraging students and staff. When their students or colleagues take a chance to *seize the moment*, such educators attempt to *be that one moment* for them, encouraging, supporting, and finding a way to help them make their dream happen.

We can never forget that our bodies are listening to everything our minds think and our mouths speak.

Expect Their Best

One of our good friends and colleagues, Salome Thomas-EL, an award-winning principal in Philadelphia and author of the bestselling book *I Choose to Stay: A Black Teacher Refuses to Desert the Inner City*, is someone who has devoted his entire life to going above and beyond in serving his students and their families. He constantly drives home the message that hard work, preparation, and lofty goals deliver results. To parents and educators, he emphasizes the value of being involved in their children's lives and serving as a positive role model. The interaction provides what he terms "the immortality of influence." In other words, the impact that a teacher or principal has on any one child can echo for eternity. Principal EL often preaches that every child deserves the opportunity for someone to be crazy about them. He isn't alone in his beliefs. In fact, it's likely that most dedicated and hardworking educators believe that all children—regardless of race, socio-economic class, ethnicity, perceived ability, or attitude—should be held to the highest standards and expectations when it comes to their academics and their behavior. As educators, we understand that having low standards and expectations would send the message to students and parents that we don't believe or don't care whether the child can learn or act appropriately. Oftentimes when teachers and principals give up on a student, it is because of a student's perceived poor attitude or poor behavior. Sadly, there are still some pockets of educators who believe that some students don't belong in a school environment due to their history of poor behavior or poor academic track record. Ironically, there are students and parents who feel the same way about some teachers and principals, believing that these educators don't truly care about their child or that they are disingenuous or openly negative.

An incident that happened early in Jimmy's career magnifies this concern. He had just encountered a student in the hallway who was visibly angry and in tears. When Jimmy asked the student what had happened to cause him to be so upset, the student simply repeated over and over that the teacher was fake. Jimmy continued to console him to try and figure out what had occurred. After a few minutes, the student explained in detail what had transpired. The student stated that he had earned a reward for turning in all his homework for the math unit and that he had been invited to dinner and an NBA game—the Milwaukee Bucks versus the Orlando Magic—with the teacher and a few other students. The young student was thrilled about seeing his favorite player, Shaquille O'Neal, play in person. The evening had been very special, and the student was finally beginning to feel as though the teacher cared about him. The next day he showed up to class not having completed his math homework from the previous night. When the teacher realized he had not finished his homework, she called him out in front of the class, telling him how disappointed she was in him for not doing his homework, especially after everything she had done for him the night before. He admitted arguing with the teacher, and this continued for a few minutes until she raised her voice and said, "Get out!"

The best educators with whom we have worked recognize that it is never about them, but rather about others, and, in most cases, about the students. They don't take things personally and they don't give up on kids, despite realizing that kids will, in fact, disappoint us at times. Why? Because they are kids, and that is what kids do. They disappoint us. Excellent educators don't fret about this; instead, they view it as an opportunity to cultivate a relationship that may not have existed previously. Rather than send a student to the hallway or to the office for not having their homework completed or for being disrespectful, they choose to spend more time talking to a student to understand why. They reach out to parents to see how they can partner together to help their child be successful. They champion for all of their students, communicating and working with other teachers, counselors, support staff, and administration to help them develop a plan for success. In the scenario described above, maybe the student didn't use his class time wisely, or perhaps he didn't understand the work, or maybe it was because he felt he deserved to take the night off after having completed his homework for the entire unit. Whatever the reason, what we do know is that the student was sent out of the classroom. The best teachers recognize that the impact they will have on any one student will be directly related to the relationships they are able to cultivate with their students. They are viewed by their students as fair, caring, approachable, empathetic, understanding, honest, and respectful. Educators who are relationship focused don't just build relationships with their students; they invest time and energy in their colleagues, parents, and, quite frankly, with all guests who enter their school.

Along the same line, principals who *go the way* strive for excellence when it comes to setting high standards for their staff. They understand the value of expecting the best from their staff as much as they expect to give their best back to their staff. However, they also recognize that not every staff member is able to bring 100 percent to their work every day. Many award-winning principals whose schools we have visited share the same, unique leadership characteristic: They spend significant time cultivating personal relationships with all their staff members so that they understand when a staff member is not at their best. Rather than judge or comment on a staff member's lack of effort on a given day, these leaders take time to invest in their team to better understand the impetus of their lackluster effort. What they have figured out over time is that these perceived shortcomings regarding performance are often the result of a much deeper personal issue, such as a troubled relationship, divorce, depression, a sick child, caring for an elderly parent, or watching a loved one die from cancer. These external events are very real and can impact even the most dedicated staff member in a way that keeps them from bringing their best. Even then, an excellent staff member's 70 percent is still relatively good, and their principal is appreciative of their efforts. As we have learned over time, one of the best barometers for determining an excellent culture is the level of empathy that exists among the staff.

> **One of the best barometers for determining an excellent culture is the level of empathy that exists among the staff.**

The best educators truly believe that no child wants to be a failure. They don't buy into the lip service that struggling learners give when they say they don't care whether they pass or not. What they do know is that the students do care, but lack the basic skills or the confidence to be successful. They also know there are other factors contributing to their sometimes extremely poor attitudes, including lack of self-discipline, work ethic, or in some cases, a refusal to overcome the challenges they may be facing. Highly committed educators realize that all of these reasons combined are related to the student not believing they can do the work and lacking the necessary skills. This combination of lack of belief and skills results in what appears to be an apathetic attitude towards the subject matter or school. In most cases, these students have simply lost their way and have given up. The best teachers go the extra mile to help them find their way back. They realize, too, that no teacher-preparation program could possibly prepare them for every peril they will undoubtedly face when working with some students and their families, but they never use this as an excuse not to keep trying. By never giving up on a child, they maintain hope that their impact will echo for eternity. Excellent educators expect the best from everyone they serve, whether students or adults. When they are not getting someone's best, they first seek to understand why, but still hold others accountable for their personal best, supporting them along the way. When it comes to expecting the very best from others, these educators know this key secret: They first have to *go the way*, expecting the best from themselves every single day. As we often say, what we model is what we get.

The Words We Say . . . or Don't Say

One of our favorite topics to discuss with educators serving in any role is that of school culture. Teachers and building-level administrators often ask what are one or two simple ideas that can really help move their organization to the next level. The fact is, no one or two things that make an organization thrive with pride can lead to a culture of excellence. Rather, a thousand little things come together to foster an environment that everyone wants to be a part of because of the way they feel when they are in that environment. When addressing these questions, we are often reminded of this quote by Annika Thor: "A conversation is so much more than words; a conversation is eyes, smiles, the silences between words."

Simple interactions impact the culture and climate of classrooms and the overall school.

Excellent educators know that it is not only the words they say that can have a lasting, positive impact on their students, but also the words they don't say that can have just as much of a profound effect on a child. Educators who go the way model the behaviors they want to see repeated: they smile a lot, share a friendly "hello" when they pass students and staff in the halls, are intentional in seeking out others and compliment their work both in writing and verbally, and engage everyone they see in genuine conversation. They say "we" and "our" instead of "I" and "my" when sharing success stories, offer moral support by attending school functions and events, congratulate students on their performances, and, most importantly, take time to listen to students and staff share what is important to them. In other words, they have come to understand that simple interactions matter, and they never pass up an opportunity to greet a student or staff member with a friendly smile or a warm greeting. Great teachers know the value of standing at their classroom door and greeting every student by name as they enter the classroom, whether it be with a smile, a handshake, fist bump or high-five! They never use the excuse that they don't have time or that they were busy doing other things like preparing for the start of class. They have a mindset that nothing is more important than time with kids. They have learned that these simple interactions impact the culture and climate of their classrooms and the overall school. Their actions suggest to students that they are important, that they matter. They leave little doubt to students and to their families that there is nothing more important than building personal relationships with their child. As Todd often says, in an excellent classroom, every student feels like the teacher's favorite student.

In an excellent classroom, every student feels like the teacher's favorite student.

We have all experienced walking into a variety of business establishments, whether it be a bank, a car dealership, a doctor's office, a grocery store, or a convenience store. We often hear others joke about the infamous store greeting that many of us have heard at one time or another: "Welcome to Wal-Mart." Interestingly enough, many other businesses have now copied this idea by providing their own version of the Wal-Mart greeter, and we say, "Why not?" Most people appreciate a friendly smile and a warm welcome. For many years, Hy-Vee, Inc., a Midwestern grocery-store chain, has had its own positive catchphrase: "Where there's a helpful smile . . . in every aisle!" Although its prices may be higher across the board than some competitors, the grocery-store chain believes that by providing excellent service in a friendly environment, customers will make the decision to shop with them rather than with their lower-priced competitors. In the business world, the way customers feel when they enter a store can be the difference between success and bankruptcy. Chick-fil-A is another example of a company that believes in service first, and that heartfelt hospitality can even make the food taste better. Today, the company is the second largest quick-service chain in the country.[1] They aim to have a positive influence on every individual who visits their restaurants. Dan Cathy, president of Chick-fil-A, has an interesting—and we think laudable—belief about the company's stance on serving their customers and their employees:

The word "restaurant" means "place of restoration," and we think of Chick-fil-A as an oasis where people can be restored. We strive to treat people better than the place down the street. One way we do that is by remembering that we're all people with a lot of emotional things going on that don't necessarily show on the surface, so we try to offer amenities and kindness that minister to the heart.

Upon reflection, this would serve as one heck of a mission statement for most schools today. Imagine walking in and having this sign in every office and every classroom in your school. Well, although the sign may not be literally in place, there are schools that live out this belief statement every day and the benefit is that students and staff feel valued and appreciated.

One school we have visited often has students serving as the frontline people in all of the school offices. When asked why this was the case, the principal stated it was done intentionally to send a subtle, though powerful, message that the school was about students first. This change brought about multiple benefits to the students and the school, including helping students develop their soft skills by dealing with parents and the public over the phone and face to face. Parents and guests seemed to enjoy seeing a smiling student face when entering the office; even more noticeable was that adults seemed to be on their best behavior when greeted by a student, even if they were unhappy or had a complaint when they first arrived. Another benefit resulting from students working in the office areas was they were able to see firsthand all of the interactions that occurred there throughout the day, providing them a better understanding and a stronger appreciation of the work that must be done to run a school effectively. They, in turn, would share this with other students and parents, giving everyone a student's perspective on the inner workings of a school. It was obvious to anyone who entered this school that students were valued and respected.

One issue all three of us experienced on a regular basis as building leaders was dealing with situations in which, quite frankly, an adult at the school had erred in their dealings with students. When teachers, support staff, and principals are dealing with students non-stop every minute of every day, there will be moments when even the best educators mismanage a situation, either by coming across as insensitive, using a harsher tone than necessary, being inflexible, or simply exhibiting obvious frustration and impatience. We are not perfect, but excellent educators never use the instances when they make a mistake as a reason not to expect better from themselves in the future and to monitor more closely what they say and how they say it moving forward. Such experiences helped us appreciate what excellent teachers did to make things right again by modeling the importance of apologizing to a student or colleague. It was not uncommon for them to ask for forgiveness because they knew that offering students sincere apologies and asking for forgiveness were not necessarily the norm; they wanted to model for them that it should be. The message they demonstrated is that when people make mistakes—and we all do—oftentimes all that is needed to resolve the situation is a sincere apology on the part of one individual and sincere forgiveness on the part of another. Our kids need to learn this important lesson. The best educators teach it by modeling it. By apologizing for a mistake, these educators ultimately earn more credibility and trust from their students. Leading is never about coming out on top of the conversation, or having to be right, or having the last word. On the contrary, excellent educators understand that there are two ways to get in the last word: apologize or accept someone's apology. The best educators just get it. They know that the words they say and the words they don't say leave a lasting impact on a child or a fellow educator.

The Hours We Keep

We suspect there is not an educator alive who has not at one time or another hid behind the standard line, "I don't have time to..." The hard truth is that we determine what we have time for and what we don't have time for. All of us can dig down deep enough to find the time when something matters a great deal to us. Walk down any school hallway at 4:00 p.m. on a school day and you will see excellence. Sometimes that excellence is disguised as an adult sitting with students in a classroom and assisting them by working on math problems, editing papers, reviewing lines for a school play, re-taking an exam, working on spelling words, practicing a musical instrument or grabbing an extra voice lesson, planning for a service project, or doing one final test run on a science project. We say "disguise" because excellent educators don't spend countless hours working with students on their "own" time because they expect any kind of special recognition. Rather, they do it because they see themselves as servant leaders and are simply there to do what they do best: work with and invest time in students and colleagues. Indeed, the best of the best recognize that in order to excel at a high level takes an enormous commitment and a work ethic that is second to none. Educators who are passionate and committed are not afraid to extend themselves beyond what others might consider a regular work week. They believe that making the greatest impact they possibly can when working with students and teachers will by all means require them to sometimes work long into the evening, or even weekends. By all accounts, we are the only profession whose members do a year's worth of work in nine months and then double back during the summer months to invest even more time in our craft. *Whew!* No wonder such educators are considered some of the hardest-working and most underpaid professionals in the workforce today! The mindset of many great educators we have worked with, when questioned about why they do what they do, usually results in one of two responses. One, they do it for the kids. Two, they never want to quit working because they are afraid if they do, they might miss that *aha!* moment, or worse yet, give up right before the miracle happens.

Inspired educators have come to accept the reality that it takes a tremendous investment on their part if they want to perform at a high level. Work viewed as excellent requires a mindset that screams, "I am all in!" Over the course of many years, we have been blessed to work not only with countless devoted teachers who were all in, but also secretaries, food-service workers, paraprofessionals, parent volunteers, and custodial staff who devoted long hours to ensure positive experiences for all students. Here are just a few of the common characteristics that separated these folks in terms of their drive to *go the way* of committing their time to model excellence. These staff members:

1. Believe in giving back

2. Invest in others every day

3. Find time to greet children every day

4. Possess a "Whatever it Takes" mindset

5. Want to be pushed by others

6. Find a connection with kids each day

7. Go out of their way to share a bit of kindness with others

8. Accept that teaching is calling, not a job

9. Take time to show gratitude to others

10. Make time for others, but also make time for themselves

Many school leaders who exemplify excellence work extremely long hours out of habit. They take personal responsibility and do all they can to ensure that the hours they commit directly impact students and staff in a positive way. They typically are among the first to arrive and the last to leave. One principal we worked with shared that she arrives early each day in order to walk the school building before her day gets started. She described the many times she is able to walk and talk with her building custodians, visit with the cooks before the day begins, get to really know them as people, learn about their families, understand their daily tasks, support them in their daily challenges, and see the pride they take in going above and beyond in their work. "Some of the most underappreciated staff members in our school are our cooks and custodians," she shared. "I never take the work they do and the hours they commit for granted, and it is important to me that they know I care." Along the same lines, she shared how she tries to model the same approach after hours by visiting with teachers and students. She does her best to show her appreciation by acknowledging their hard work, even after the day has ended. She makes an effort to stop by athletic practices, music rehearsals, and, every now and then, even jumps in to help a struggling student with their homework. "Sure, I keep long hours as a building leader, but spending time with students and staff and investing in their activities and work is not only important, but also rewarding," she said. "In fact, it is probably what keeps me energized and looking forward to coming back to work every day, more excited than I was the day before. It never seems like a job to me. It's just who I am."

We have learned from spending time with school personnel as well as from our own experiences in recent decades that the job of an educator can be taxing. We share this with you not because we want to deter you from this wonderful profession or because we want those outside the field of education to take pity on us. No, we share this to affirm everyone out there who may be questioning themselves about whether they can continue to maintain these long hours. After all, most educators we know can't imagine themselves doing anything else and certainly know that even if they could, it would not be as rewarding. Education is in our DNA. It is not merely a job to us, but a lifestyle—a lifestyle driven by the belief that the hours we keep allow us to truly make a difference in the lives of others.

Tell the Truth

A new teacher hesitantly asks his principal after a walk-through, "What did you think today after you walked through my classroom?"

"It was great. The kids seemed engaged and interested in what you were sharing," responds the principal.

On the surface, this may appear to be a typical response, or what you might expect a conversation to look like between a teacher and principal after a quick walk-through. But let us ask: What did this response really say? Did the principal really mean it was great, or was she just being cordial? What was great about it? Were all students engaged? Were they really all interested? Or was this just her polite way of avoiding pointing out some concerns? Moreover, what is the teacher thinking? Is the teacher wondering if the principal really did think it was great, or was she just trying to be nice and was afraid that his feelings would be hurt if she told him the truth?

In most schools, people are really good at being congenial, but not necessarily collegial.

Tell the truth. Seems simple, doesn't it? But in schools around the country, conversations like these happen daily in schools between teachers and administrators, as well as teachers and students. We have found that in most schools, people are really good at being congenial, but not necessarily collegial. In other words, many of the conversations remain on the surface and really never go to a deeper dialogue for fear of hurting someone's feelings or upsetting a colleague. It is common practice to hear staff talk amongst each other at a morning department meeting or after-school grade-level meeting about a school event, how their weekend was, or bantering over the likelihood of the Chicago Cubs ever winning back-to-back World Series championships. Although perfectly normal and even healthy for overall school climate, what is also needed are conversations that help both students and staff become better. Conversations that are genuine. Conversations that are about performance, instruction, school climate issues, school policies. Discussions that are about grading practices, classroom management, family engagement, or addressing inappropriate student behavior. The best teachers and school leaders we know are not afraid to have candid conversations that speak the truth around these domains. They exhibit a willingness to go further with the discussion in order to encourage more questions, truthful dialogue, and reflection, because they understand that without reflection there cannot be growth. Courageous leaders are not afraid to address underperformance, and caring teachers don't shy away from telling the truth when it comes to working with their students. Excellent leaders, like excellent teachers, recognize when a teacher or student has not given their best effort. However, rather than admonish their efforts, they challenge them appropriately to do better. Both have tremendously high expectations and when those expectations are not met, rather than say "good job" and leave it at that, they may follow up with something along the lines of, "What did you like about your performance, and what would you do differently if you were given another chance?" You see, excellence never settles; it is never satisfied with just good. "Good enough" is not a part of a great educator's vernacular.

It is important to understand that whether we are working with students or working with adults, we don't do them any favors when we are not honest with our feedback. Of course, great teachers and great administrators have figured out that the key is to get others to see the value of feedback for themselves so students and staff don't feel attacked or defeated. Great teachers manage the conversation in a way that leaves students feeling challenged and invigorated to come back and try it again because someone took the time to explain to them, in detail, what they did well.

Jeff recently had a conversation with a teacher who explained that she never includes a grade when she reviews a student's work for the first time and also makes sure to provide detailed feedback with examples in writing. Why? Because she views a student's first submission of work as the first attempt at success; she believes it is her duty to provide meaningful and truthful feedback in order to push her students towards excellence. "My students know that I won't allow them to be satisfied with a passing mark or accept a mediocre paper. No, in this class, they know I love them and I am all about being truthful with my feedback, but I do so in a caring way in order to help them grow."

Excellent leaders have learned that it is best to address staff members by being truthful and upfront with them when they are not meeting expectations. It is not fair, nor is it appropriate, to keep staff guessing in terms of expectations because the building leader is afraid to address legitimate concerns or to state what he or she truly believes is the best solution for all students and staff. When some staff members are not submitting grades on time, not actively supervising kids on the playground, not showing up promptly for team meetings, or are treating colleagues disrespectfully, strong and caring leaders do not shirk their responsibility; they address the behavior. Not only do they address it, but they do so in a way that is fair and consistent, leaving the staff member feeling supported because the correction was done in a way that made them feel heard and understood, and more importantly, they were left with a clear understanding of what is expected of them.

Regardless of the difficulty of the conversation, excellent educators never avoid these crucial conversations. When they do so, they unfortunately alienate their most invested students and staff members who, by their own standards and admission, thrive better in an environment that expects excellence and is not afraid to confront the truth. The job of all teachers and building and district administrators is to help their

students and their employees grow and develop in their roles as learners. This progress can only happen if they are honest and accept the
responsibility that leadership is about helping others achieve success,
one truthful conversation at a time.

Ask for Help

Several years ago, the three of us were sitting together at dinner
and sharing our personal stories of how we got started in education.
We realized that each of us had someone who inspired us to want to
become a teacher and, later on, we were each mentored by someone
who believed in our abilities to be a school principal. Not only did
these individuals inspire us, they helped us all along our journey by
encouraging us, sharing personal teaching and learning moments
from their own experience, delegating meaningful tasks to help build
our confidence, inviting us to serve on building leadership teams, providing opportunities to facilitate faculty meetings, leading professional
development, and trusting us. At dinner that evening, we discussed our
concerns about the shortage of quality support for principals once they
complete their educational leadership programs. We came to the con-
clusion that one of the biggest challenges building principals face today
is finding that special someone to coach them once they are assigned
to a building. During that same conversation, we also discussed some
hard truths about the mindset of many building leaders, including why
they struggle. By the end of the evening, we agreed on the simple truth
that many of these leaders struggle because they refuse to ask for help.

The practice of not asking for help is as common among building
and district administrators as it is among teachers and students. On
the one hand, a new employee or struggling student may feel embar-
rassed to ask for help. Admitting that they need help may make them
feel ignorant, incompetent, or incapable of performing at the expected
level. When we assign others responsibilities and trust them to fulfill

such responsibilities—whether that means completing a homework assignment for a student or managing the school safety plan for an assistant principal—we have to understand that it might be difficult for some to admit they are unsure of their understanding of the task or their ability to complete it. Many are fearful of disappointing those who believed in them. For anyone harboring any feeling of self-doubt, this fear can send them into a tailspin. If you are faced with an endless number of responsibilities, some of which seem daunting, and you are trying to figure it all out on your own, here's a simple solution: Stop trying to do it alone. Ask for help.

Stop trying to do it alone. Ask for help.

The majority of educators we have met and connected with are willing to assist others at a moment's notice, without judgment, and in a confidential manner that maintains a professional working relationship. However, the real work that needs to be done is convincing educators to model for their colleagues and students that, regardless of whether you are a first-year principal, a fifth-year principal, a twenty-year veteran teacher, a middle-school student, or a junior in high school, it is okay to ask others for assistance. There isn't a single educator in the business today who didn't need someone else's help to get to where they are at today. The same holds true for our students. Students need to be reminded in a caring and loving way that it is OK to ask for help opening their lockers, finding a classroom or where the bus pick-up will take place, and figuring out what time lunch starts and ends. As the adults in charge of caring for children, we also can anticipate, based on our experiences, where students will struggle and then we must be proactive in order to avoid them having to ask these questions and experiencing the anxiety that often comes with it.

Great teachers cultivate a classroom environment where students feel comfortable asking for help. Students look forward to spending time with the teacher to learn the material because they genuinely enjoy the camaraderie that comes with it. Caring teachers, through their words and their actions, have a way of building a student's confidence level. They eliminate the stigma of asking for help by ensuring that asking questions and seeking help become the norm for "how we do things around here." These educators have the same effect on their colleagues. When they see a teammate struggling to keep up with a new grading software, getting stuck on lesson planning, dealing with student behavior issues, or needing someone to cover their classroom for a few minutes because they haven't had a chance to go to the bathroom all morning, they are quick to offer help and, more importantly, they are sincere in their offer. The best of the best are always ready to support their colleagues, regardless of the time commitment.

Excellent principals also foster these types of environments and establish a clear philosophy with all office employees that everyone is responsible for establishing a culture and climate where everyone feels welcomed and valued and looks forward to coming to the office, where their questions will be answered in a pleasant manner and their needs will be attended to with a heart-warming smile. In a school of excellence, you will see students and staff lingering in the office areas because the people in that office have established a reputation of being available to serve and tend to the needs of everyone who enters at a moment's notice. Great principals are also proactive when working with their office staff and their own administrative colleagues when it comes to encouraging them to never hesitate to seek out assistance. They infuse a sense of comfort in others by modeling themselves that asking for help is the best way to build trust and confidence in others. A servant leader not only gives, but she takes, by asking for help from students, teachers, support staff, parents, and central office staff when she feels the need is there.

Excellent educators are never too proud to say, "I need help," or "I don't know how to do this." Their openness communicates to everyone that struggling is part of learning and that the first step to becoming a lifelong learner is asking for help and the second step is accepting it. By asking for and accepting help, great educators foster a school culture in which the community members feel like family—a family that loves and supports one another unconditionally.

Stay the Course

In the board game *Monopoly*, the object is simple. It is to send every other player into bankruptcy. It is important to remember that it is not to amass the most wealth. You could have only one dollar in cash at the end and still win the game. Avoiding the small green houses and the big red hotels can seem like a hopeless endeavor, especially when you are one roll away from landing on Boardwalk. But if you want to win, you must stay the course, regardless of the amount of properties you land on or how many times you get sent to jail.

Just like in *Monopoly*, dedicated teachers and leaders keep their focus and don't get caught up in short-term losses.

Educators who strive for excellence stay the course and know that by doing so, they will eventually pass "Go" and collect the $200 they might need at the moment to remain in the game. Just like in *Monopoly*, dedicated teachers and leaders keep their focus and don't get caught up in short-term losses. The best educators stay the course and recognize that the long-term results they desire for their classrooms and school buildings will eventually come—even if they must wait to first pass

"Go." Experience has taught them that even if they don't see the immediate results of their work, they will eventually—as long as they stay the course.

Many of the best teachers and principals we know accept the notion that each day they walk through their school doors, they must be committed to making a difference in the lives of their students and staff. They remain steadfast in facing the challenges, accepting the failures, and honoring the successes because they understand that none of these are a final destination. They have deduced that these experiences will continue to shape their inner core values and strengthen their resolve in their daily work. They have come to accept that the work of an educator is an ongoing and ever-changing process, and that success is often slow in arriving.

On a recent visit to a school, Jimmy was introduced to a young lady who was in her second year of teaching special education. She worked with students who had both severe cognitive and physical disabilities. Each morning, she greeted her students and their parents in the parking lot and, with support from her teacher aides, assisted the students into school. In addition to the daily academic lessons and regular physical and recreation activities, the teacher spent time feeding, clothing, and sometimes bathing her students. At other times, the students' needs required her to physically lift and stretch her students as part of their Individualized Educational Plan (IEP) goals. She often attended class in the general education classrooms with her students so she could participate with her students in a lab experiment, a music lesson, or history lesson. She loved seeing her students' big, wide smiles each time a classmate greeted them with a high-five or they got to participate in a group project. When Jimmy left the classroom, he asked the principal about the teacher that he had just observed. The principal explained, "She is one of my best teachers, even though she is just in her second year. She loves her children and cares for them as though they were her own. What I am most proud of is that she is one of our graduates. In fact, she is back working in the same classroom where she worked as a student assistant in our 'Best Buddies' program. During her job interview, she shared that she never stopped thinking about the students and felt that if she came back, she could make a difference. Most students would maybe have gone in a different direction after such a challenging experience, but not her. She is special. I guess you can say that she stayed the course." Some of the most passionate teachers that we have encountered in our work with schools serve in the area of special education. Our experiences have been filled with nurturing, loving, and dedicated educators who believe that all children—including our children with special needs—deserve opportunities to maximize their growth potential, regardless of their circumstances.

Excellent educators go out of their way to stay the course, regardless of the complexity of their role or the fact that the variables are always changing. Inevitably, even the best principals and teachers will hit times of struggle as they deal with the emotional toll inherent with caring so deeply about their work and the people it impacts. However, rather than veering off course, they become fueled and energized by those challenges. They push forward, keeping their focus on the new goals in front of them. In the end, they trust that there will be moments, days, and events that will appear as though they have finally made it, but only if they have selected the right route and stayed the course.

The Way We Respond

Have you ever reached out to someone, asking for help of any kind, only to be disappointed by the response—or even lack of a response? Excellent teachers and excellent school leaders know the importance of responding, including both *when* and *how* to respond. We are honestly shocked at how often some people in our profession fail at the easiest part of this formula: They choose to not respond in *any* way to some emails, phone messages, or communications via social media they receive. We certainly understand how busy everyone is; we are busy, too. In fact, we suspect that the very best teachers and leaders in any school district are even busier than their mediocre colleagues. Still, they do something amazing whenever they receive a legitimate call for assistance of any kind: They respond. Every time. Without fail. Excellent educators never ignore a communication from a parent, colleague, student, or member of their P²LN. Sometimes, when they respond, it is simply to say they are honestly unable to help with a given problem. If it is a request about an area in which they have no expertise, they may try to connect the seeker with someone who can help. But at the very least, they respond immediately, letting the person know that the communication has been received. They may even write a quick a note, telling the sender that they will respond in greater detail by the end of the day or in twenty-four hours. Although they cannot provide a complete response at the moment, they choose to immediately acknowledge and honor the person who reached out. Everyone reading this book has likely, at some point in life, felt the sting of disappointment that comes with a complete lack of response. Maybe you have contacted someone about something you thought was important, and waited days (or longer) for a reply. If so, you know what it is like to feel ignored. Excellent educators also know how it feels when someone ignores their communication. Moreover, they know how it feels when someone does respond immediately and lends a hand. Knowing firsthand the difference between the two feelings, they always choose the latter in their own practices. It is definitely challenging keeping up with every communication we receive. Excellent educators are challenged with this, too, but this is yet another challenge they accept and address. By *going the way* when it comes to deciding *whether* to respond, they are modeling for others that this is important.

Obviously, *if* and *when* we respond is important; the best educators respond to every legitimate communication and do so promptly. Equally important is *how* they respond. There is a saying: "You can't live a positive life with a negative mind." The same holds true for educators and schools in how they respond when they are faced with small, or even significant, demands. We can't cultivate a positive school culture if the people who work in the school have a negative attitude when it comes to how they respond to timelines, requests, mandates, union members, new initiatives, emails, phone calls, students, parents, and a whole plethora of other facets they encounter on a daily basis. One of the biggest challenges for school leaders today is figuring out how to help their personnel remain positive on a daily basis when faced with constant demands on their time, especially when those demands are accompanied by short timelines. Excellent educators have discovered that neither their failures nor their successes in meeting those demands defines who they are; rather their choice in *how* they respond is the factor that dictates their attitude and ultimately defines them.

First and foremost, great educators maintain a positive mindset regardless of the situation or the circumstances in which they find themselves. They understand that their main responsibility is to ensure that the "customer" leaves feeling content about the response. By taking this approach and keeping the focus on ensuring that the other person is satisfied, they, too, find a sense of fulfillment. Successful educators feed off the energy of others' sense of accomplishment. This cycle then continues with each interaction. For example, when a building principal receives a call late in the evening at home from a parent, she makes sure to stress that it is okay and that they are not being a bother. When receiving an email from a concerned parent on a Sunday, rather than wait and cause the parent to be stressed over the situation for the next twenty-four hours, she responds immediately in a manner that makes the parent feel grateful for the quick response. When she stays late at the office and a teacher (who is also working late) stops by and asks if she has a minute, she always says "yes"—even though she knows that the minute will eventually lead to thirty.

Excellent educators realize the importance of responding promptly and positively to every communication they receive.

Many of the outstanding school leaders we know have shared with us they prefer to respond with a personal phone call rather than an email. In some cases, some principals even shared they provide their personal cell numbers when necessary in order to help out a parent who is in a bad predicament. When responding face to face, they are keenly aware of their body language, disposition, tone, and mindset. Equally important, they pay sharp attention to the body language and responsiveness of those to whom they are responding, be it a visitor, parent, colleague, or student. When an excellent teacher is confronted with a frustrated student or with an irrational parent, he is able to maintain his composure and remain calm, never taking things personally because deep down he knows in this moment, whatever is causing the other person to behave in this manner has nothing really to do with him. Excellent educators realize the importance of responding promptly and positively to every communication they receive. By choosing to consistently respond in these ways, they set a clear standard for others in terms of *the way to respond*.

TEACH 4, LEAD 4, LEARN 4

Teachers and leaders with whom we have worked and who stand out as truly excellent exhibit a clear pattern of modeling each day what it means to *go the way* professionally and personally. They know that others are listening to what they say, but more importantly, they are watching what they do. Consequently, they are keenly aware of their own actions as well as the actions of others, realizing that the root of their success will be based on the example they set. Our very best teachers and leaders aim to be that one moment for their students and colleagues. They are intentional in their efforts to be present in their interaction and always expect the best from others by emphasizing the importance of hard work and setting lofty goals. They know a conversation is so much more than words and what they say or don't say can have a lasting positive impact on their students. They inherently work long hours, but never track the hours they keep because they view their work as a lifestyle rather than a job. Of course, they have figured out that it is always best to tell the truth when expectations are not being met in order to support others in their quest for success. Along the same lines, they aren't afraid to ask for help, recognizing that struggling is part of learning. Regardless of the challenges that will undoubtedly come their way, they stay the course and remain constant as they move forward, never swaying from their path. Finally, they know that it is not only when they respond, but how they respond that will determine their long-term success.

Teach 4

Here are four educators who we believe stand out as exemplars for *Going the Way*:

1. Rachel Cuppy (@rcuppy1) serves as a special education teacher at Bettendorf High School. Rachel has spent her entire career working with students with severe behavior disorders. In her role serving students with special needs, Rachel recognizes that if she is going to be successful in helping her students experience success, she must continue to reach out and *ask for help* from support staff, general education teachers, administration, and parents.

During the past sixteen years, I have learned a lot about teaching. I started my career in a small school that had very few students and staff. Now I teach in a building with more than 1,400 students and many staff members in every department. My early days of teaching were tough. I was a new teacher who worked in a building that had a "do-it-yourself" culture. In that first year, I often wondered why so many people loved my chosen profession. Teaching was difficult, and I felt alone.

Today, my career is my passion. I have learned to ask for help when I am struggling. Gone is the young and insecure me who worried that people would think that I was weak if I did not have all the answers. I have been fortunate to work with leaders and coworkers who made me feel comfortable asking for help when I needed it. I no longer feel like I have to be the expert in all areas of my career. My students benefit from not only my knowledge, but also the knowledge of everyone around me. Asking for help has led me to a deeper understanding of learning disabilities, technology, personality conflicts, and even cultural differences that I would not have understood without the expertise of others. By watching me interact with my co-teacher, para-educators, secretaries, and custodians, my students learn that it is normal and beneficial to ask for help. They learn that asking for help often leads to options and collaboration in learning and living. Today, I am more confident in my teaching abilities than I have ever been before. I have learned that I cannot do it all by myself, and no one expects me to!

2. Bill Ferriter (@plugusin) is a sixth-grade teacher in North Carolina. He is an author, a noted edublogger, and serves as a senior fellow for the *Teacher Leaders Network*. Bill is a leader in technology-enhanced learning practices that are tied directly to the instructional standards that matter. Throughout his career, Bill has continued to *stay the course* when it comes to decisions that impact teaching and learning.

For me, there's really nothing difficult about staying the course in the face of the constant changes and challenges that add complexity to the work of classroom teachers. That's because I know full well that the future success of every student that rolls through my classroom door depends, to some degree, on my willingness to stay the course. Choosing not to adapt—not to tinker with my practices, not to identify and adjust to new priorities and realities, not to move forward regardless of the obstacles standing in my path—means choosing to fail the kids in my classroom, and that's a choice I'm not willing to make.

I've also learned that I can play a role in the professional successes of my closest colleagues—and that they play a role in mine. We tinker together in hopes of finding the practices that make the biggest impact on student learning. We adjust to new priorities and realities together, recognizing that each of us brings a unique set of instructional strengths to the planning table. And we move forward together, making the obstacles standing in our way a little less daunting. Staying the course is always easier when you recognize that you don't have to walk alone. In the end, I see staying the course as an act of service to the students in my classroom and to the colleagues that I care the most about—and service to others always makes sustained effort worthwhile.

3. Derek Dixon (@Mr_DerekDixon) serves as a social studies teacher at Tama Middle School in Tama, Iowa. He previously taught social studies in English Valley, Iowa. Derek is a teacher who is passionate about all aspects of his work. He believes that his mission as an educator is to model the behaviors that he expects from his students and works to create a classroom environment in which both he and his students *expect their best.*

At the beginning of the school year, I have my students create expectations for themselves. I call them "expectations" because these are things that students can live up to. I also have my students explain in writing how they will achieve each one, and let them know that this is how I will hold them accountable for reaching their potential. I realize that my actions must model what it is that I am asking my students to do, so I share with them the expectations I create for myself for the school year. I share the following professional and personal expectations with them:

1. *Always put students first.*

2. *Continue growing and learning as a teacher and leader.*

3. *Continue working on improving my physical health.*

I feel as though it is important to model the types of behaviors I am expecting from my students.

I have made it my daily mission to do what is best for kids and be that positive role model and champion for them. This is not an easy task, however, and it can be physically and mentally draining at times. The important thing to remember is that your actions and how you act around both your students and staff can really go a long way toward making a difference in the lives of others. I have realized that just simply smiling at students and saying "hello" in the hallways can make a world of difference in trying to establish a positive culture and climate. I've also realized that people want to know that they matter. Both students and staff want to feel as though they have a place and are cared for while they are here. "You Matter" advocate Angela Maiers states, "If you don't first secure students' hearts, you don't have a shot at their brains." I strive to live by that statement and model that consistently every day.

4. **Ben Feight (@FeightB)** is an elementary teacher in the Cedar Rapids Community School District in Iowa. In 2014, Ben was named the Iowa Technology Educator of the Year. Ben serves as a tremendous teaching resource for educators who want to infuse technology into their teaching. With such a constant demand on his time, Ben can

relate to challenges associated with *the way we respond*. As a result, he monitors his actions in this area to ensure he responds effectively and efficiently.

During my past six years of teaching, I have learned how vital communication is to the success of all stakeholders in education. The biggest part of achieving effective communication is trust. I am always available for my students, families, and colleagues. I make this clear to all of them before the first day of school even begins. Being a digitally connected educator, I have multiple ways for families to contact me if they can't find me "face to face." I want the people who come in contact with me to know that I will always respond to them when I have the available time to devote all my attention to that situation. This may seem like a juggling act at times, but it is very reassuring for a parent to know I will always respond to their email or various social media messages they might send me. I also send out positive text messages and emails to parents and staff members if I absolutely can't talk with them face to face just to let them know I am still thinking about them. All staff and parents have a mutual understanding with me that the students come first, so if I am teaching or working with a student, I will respond to them after I am done with the student. One of the easiest ways I've found to build trust with my students is just a simple, genuine smile and "Hello!" as they are walking into my classroom each morning. When a child is crying on the playground, just sitting down on the ground next to her can go a long way. Letting students know you will try to get on their "level" at an elementary age will build trust, and that will lead to effective communication.

Lead 4

Here are four educators currently serving primarily in educational leadership roles. We believe they stand out as exemplars for *Going the Way*:

1. Jon Harper (@Jonharper70bd) serves as assistant principal at Sandy Hill Elementary in Cambridge, Maryland. Prior to becoming an administrator, he served as a math coach and an elementary-school teacher. For seven years, he ran a Young Gentleman's Club that was aimed at helping young men reach their full potential, striving each day to *be that one moment* for his students and staff.

Here's a challenge: Pick a few students tomorrow and do everything you can to see that the first few seconds or minutes of their day are freakin' amazing. Then, at the end of the day, try to check in with their teacher, or even better, check in with them.

I believe that my first encounters with students each day should be magnificent. I must let them know that I am ecstatic that they came to school. I can start this off with a bright smile, a high-five, or maybe even a warm hug. I must always remember that just a few thoughtful seconds may determine how the rest of a student's day goes. For better or for worse. It is not my job or my right to immediately point out their shortcomings. Maybe they didn't do their homework. I need to find a way to help them get it completed. Maybe they are angry when they first enter the building or classroom. I must find a way to calm them down. At the very least, I can give them an ear to listen. It is my job to serve them. Not vice versa.

Additionally, I try to make sure that my first encounter with staff members has nothing to do with school. Why? Because the rest of their day is going to be about school. Because most likely, a portion of their previous evening was about school. And because I mustn't ever forget that school is what they do, it is not who they are. So, I ask about their family. Find out how they are feeling. I show them that I know more about them than their data and what lesson they're on. Of course it is my job to know these things. But who wants to begin their day like that? I sure don't! And you can be certain that your staff doesn't.

2. **Jennifer Hogan (@Jennifer_Hogan)** is assistant principal at Hoover High School in Hoover, Alabama, who has also served as a science teacher, coach, and principal. In her various professional roles, Jennifer has learned that *the hours we keep* can threaten to overwhelm us. Still, she manages to find time for her students, colleagues, friends, and family.

As a school leader, the hours we keep is an appropriate topic that should be examined, reviewed, and capitalized on. I know that in my experience as a school leader, time is a precious commodity that doesn't seem to be equally utilized among educators. Bob Bowman, the coach who helped Michael Phelps achieve extraordinary results, says that we must be "students of the profession." When I reflect on the time I have put into my profession, it includes learning from those I work with in person, plus reading journals, blog posts, books, and articles, attending conferences, participating in Twitter chats, and other activities that relate to education. Almost all of my free time is spent learning more about my profession, but it never seems like a burden because it is something that I am truly passionate about. I have immersed myself in instructional practices, sociology, leadership theories and practices, and psychology. Because of that, I have been able to develop a strong personal vision for myself as well as for the educators around me. The extra time I've spent research-ing, listening, reading, implementing, observing, and learning have been the difference that has separated me from those who are just "doing a job," or meeting a job description. To make a difference and leave a legacy, I truly believe it takes educators who are willing to do the behind-the-scenes work and be students of the profession.

Here's the ironic thing, though: Although, like most educators around the world, I devote many, many hours to our noble pro-fession, well above and beyond what is "required," it seems as if in some ways, the harder I work, the more time I make for myself. My colleagues who work the hardest somehow always seem to have just a little bit left in their tank for their families and for outside interests, as well as their schools. It is almost as if the long work hours not only energize them, but force them to prioritize the tasks in their lives and the hours in their days.

3. Malynn Rodriguez (@malynn_r) is a principal at Odessa Kilpatrick Elementary School in Katy, Texas. At Odessa Kilpatrick Elementary, relationships come first and rise above all other priorities. Malynn knows that one way to create and maintain positive relationships with all members of the school community is to carefully monitor *the words we say... and don't say.*

One of the very first life lessons I learned as a building principal is that everyone who enters our school has a story. I pass teachers, assistants, students, and even parents in the halls and everyone and everything seems to look great. But what I quickly came to realize is that just because things appear fine on the outside, does not mean there are not often numerous struggles happening on the inside. Because we do not have the ability to completely compartmentalize our emotions, we end up bringing pieces of these struggles with us to the classroom. Yet, I have been humbled and amazed by teachers and students working to give their very best while in the midst of a personal crisis. This is one of the many reasons why I believe relationships are so crucial. We must have meaningful experiences with each other, celebrate with each other, laugh with each other, know when others are hurting, and, sometimes, cry with each other. It is also important that we say the right things to each other—and not say things that are counterproductive to success. Developing these types of relationships takes time. As a leader, I know it is imperative that I model the importance of investing time in others. Strong relationships matter; without them, we literally have nothing.

I have also learned that it is vital that our kids have several "go-to, count-on" adults at our school that they know they can rely upon for help, support, guidance, and a listening ear. Our students need to know that they have someone in their corner: someone who cares, someone who will make himself available, and someone who will never give up on them no matter what. We conduct student interviews to get a baseline on student connectivity, voice, and dreams, as well as the students' opinions of teachers, principals, and our school. What I've learned is that when students are given the opportunity, they provide candid and insightful responses. We have used the information gleaned from these interviews to implement positive changes on our campus. We will continue to ask, review, and revise our practices at Odessa Kilpatrick Elementary to benefit our students. Our school is not a perfect school, and I am not a perfect school leader. However, with all that we do, we ask every single time, "What is best for our kids?" This question has to be at the root of all that we do as educators and leaders, and that makes them among the most important words we say each day!

4. **Dwight Carter (@Dwight_Carter)** is principal at New Albany High School in New Albany, Ohio. Prior to that, he served as principal at Gahanna Lincoln High School and was recognized as a 2013 Digital Principal of the Year by the National Association of Secondary School Principals. Dwight also coauthored *What's in Your Space? 5 Steps to Better School and Classroom Design.* As principal, Dwight's mission is to positively change lives and impact futures; one way he does so is simply to *tell the truth.*

In my experience, it can difficult at times to tell the truth because I don't take pleasure in hurting the feelings of others, especially when talking about their craft, their field of expertise, or something they are so passionate about. I consider myself a "words" guy, meaning I am energized and my tank is filled by words of encouragement or

*affirmation; therefore, I tend to do the same for others. The unfortu-
nate thing about this is that I have withheld constructive criticism of
others in order to spare their feelings or to not squelch their enthusiasm. This has left me feeling frustrated by their lack of effective
performance or a lack of change in their behavior. It has even gotten
to the point where a wall is put up between us, which further exas-
perates my feelings of frustration.*

*However, if I want to lead for excellence, I have to reflect on my
experiences. It wasn't until recently that I realized it's my own fault
that I have felt this way because I did not tell the truth about what I
observed in their performance, behavior, or final product. I was not
only hesitant to "speak the truth in love," but I flat-out lied to them
about their performance. In the end, it hurt our ability to effectively
meet the needs of students, it hurt my credibility in terms of being a
courageous leader, and it created a bit more dysfunction within our
school organization.*

*The situation nearly got to the level of an administrator review,
which simply means that one of my superiors would have to facilitate a meeting between me and the other staff members to help us
resolve the conflict. Thankfully, I was able to set up a meeting with
the others involved, listen attentively to how I made them feel due to
my lack of clear expectations, evasive communication, and lack of
empathy. I was also able to share my observations, perspective, and
the truth about their performance. In the end, we did not necessarily
agree on everything we discussed, but we left feeling that we understood each other. All of this could have been avoided over a year ago
if had I simply told the truth, provided coaching and support, and
celebrated their success over time. It is not always comfortable, but
being honest with each other about our performance and our feedback is always the right thing to do.*

Learn 4

Here are four resources/tools/action steps you can use to further develop yourself and others relating to the standard we call *Going the Way*:

1. Watch this short video from Mark Scharenbroich: "Nice Bike."[2] In this video, Mark talks about the importance of making connections, and the impact these connections can have in creating customer loyalty, driving growth, performance, and cultivating team spirit.

Nice Bike

2. Read "What Are the Best Strategies for Surface to Deep Learning?"[3] In this short blog post, Peter DeWitt, author of *Collaborative Leadership: 6 Influences That Matter Most*, talks about getting students from surface-level learning to a deeper level, and then getting them to transfer that learning.

What Are the Best Strategies for Surface to Deep Learning?

3. Seek feedback. A big part of going the way is simply aligning our actions to what we are saying, or, as some people say, "walking the talk." Leaders and teachers set the tone for the school and classroom environments they lead. They do so by their actions and how they choose to positively empower and influence others. Our ability to create optimal learning environments requires us to continuously reinforce our shared values. Are you aware of the environment you are creating and whether you are going the way in that regard? Seek honest feedback from a person (colleague or student) with whom you feel comfortable, and ask whether you are going the way. Ask about how he or she perceives your "talk." Afterwards, share what your "talk" is in your view, and discuss any contradictions between the two perspectives. Ask if your "walk" is aligned with your perceived "talk." Make it a habit to periodically seek out such feedback to determine whether you are consistently modeling the behaviors and characteristics you value and hope to see others adopt.

4. Create common values statements. Consider creating a list of five values statements that everyone on the team (classroom, school, district, parent community) agrees to commit to collectively. These statements should start with the words, "We will..." and describe behaviors that team members believe important enough to state publicly and hold each other accountable for. Individual classrooms can create statements for students and teachers in their classrooms to live by. Parents can meet to create statements that they, too, agree to model consistently. Here are sample faculty values statements to get you thinking about what values are important in your own environment:

➤ *We will... work together as a team.*

➤ *We will... provide and promote a safe and orderly learning environment.*

➤ *We will... treat others with dignity and respect at all times.*

➤ *We will... hold ourselves accountable.*

➤ *We will... make decisions based on what is best for kids.*

GROW EACH DAY

Teacher growth is closely related to pupil growth. Probably nothing within a school has more impact on students in terms of skills development, self-confidence, or classroom behavior than the personal and professional growth of their teachers.
—Roland Barth

During our teaching careers, all three of us also served as athletic coaches. At that time, our coaching professional development was every bit as important to us as our teaching professional development. We found that the more we learned and grew as coaches, the more, in turn, our athletes would grow. As we implemented techniques we learned at coaching clinics into our practices and games, our players excelled. Like coaches, excellent teachers are constantly growing in any number of ways. We believe—like Barth—that this professional growth also promotes student academic growth. Here, again, we have a quote that works for both teachers and leaders, however. We believe that the growth of school leaders also significantly impacts the extent to which teachers serving in the school or district grow. A teacher's skills development, self-confidence, and even their behavior while at school are influenced by the personal and professional growth of school and district leaders, much in the same way that student growth and performance mirrors teacher growth. As mentioned earlier in this book, if pressed to boil down the primary purpose of a school to a single word, that word would be *learning*. And, although student learning is first and foremost in terms of our mission, learning must not be limited to students, but must also include all adults in the school community. We must intentionally encourage and celebrate adult learning in much the same way we celebrate student learning. Excellent teachers and leaders are passionate about inspiring others to become lifelong learners. One way they do that is by modeling lifelong learning themselves.

DEFINING THE STANDARD: GROWING FOR EXCELLENCE

The fourth standard of teaching and leading for excellence exhibited by educators with whom we have worked is all about growing, improving, believing we can always get better, and encouraging and celebrating everyone in the community for their ongoing learning and development. As in the previous chapters, we've described this standard and its indicators in the text that follows. Our one-sentence definition of *Growing Each Day* is: **Exhibiting a passion for lifelong learning and growth evidenced by individuals, teams, schools, and districts that continually strive to get better by embracing a wide variety of professional learning opportunities and encouraging those within the community to promote and embody this ideal.**

STANDARD OF EXCELLENCE #4
Excellent Teachers and Leaders Grow Each Day

Excellent teachers and leaders demonstrate lifelong learning and continuous improvement. They strive to get better each day, and work to help others within the organization do the same. They promote growth in a positive, encouraging, and supportive manner.

INDICATORS

- Asks for feedback on how their actions affect other people's performance

- Provides specific feedback to others in an effort to promote the growth of those with whom they interact

- Seeks out challenging opportunities that test their own skills and abilities

- Challenges people to try new and innovative ways to do their work

- Searches outside the formal boundaries of their own district, school, department, or classroom for innovative ways to improve what they do

- Asks, "What can we learn?" when things do not go as expected

- Experiments and takes risks, even when there is a chance of failure

- Ensures that people grow in their jobs by helping them learn new skills and supporting ongoing self-development

- Recognizes and praises others for jobs well done

- Finds ways to celebrate individual, team, and large-group accomplishments

- Seeks out a wide variety of opportunities for ongoing professional growth

- **Focuses on the question, "What do I/we need to do, and when do I/we need to do it to ensure that I/we get better and the district, school, department, or classroom gets better?" and acts intentionally to achieve these goals.**

Why It Matters

Excellent educators begin their preparation for success by acquiring the necessary knowledge and skills; next, they show others how they, too, can acquire new knowledge and skills and how the classroom, school, or district overall can collectively reach new heights if everyone is committed to ongoing growth and self-improvement. Then, they model what it is they hope and expect to see from others, whether that is best practices in the classroom, best behaviors in the hallway, or speaking in a dignified and respectful manner to everyone with whom they come in contact. In other words, amazing teachers and leaders *know the way, show the way,* and *go the way.* The final piece of the puzzle is focused on growth, including growth of almost every kind. They want their students' academic scores to improve, *and* they want to see them grow socially and emotionally. Personally, they seek to become more effective and efficient at everything they do so that they can serve students—and their peers—better tomorrow than they did today. They take careful stock of their current performance, looking at every piece of available data—including, perhaps, but certainly not limited to, standardized test results. They identify successes worthy of celebration and target areas for improvement. With clear goals established, they determine which action steps are necessary for achieving those goals. In such teachers' classrooms or such leaders' schools or districts, everyone involved knows exactly where they are, where they are going, what steps they will take to arrive there, and when they will take them. When people know where they currently stand, as well as where they are going and how they will get there, they are much more likely to accomplish great things—individually and collectively.

When establishing new goals and implementing actions to accomplish them, these educators never forget to include plans for celebrating successes along the way and recognizing those who contributed to these successes. They realize that they serve in perhaps the most noble and important profession there is and take this work seriously, putting in long hours after school, on weekends, and even during vacations. Knowing this to be the case, they also make it a point to find the joy in what they do and the people with whom they work. They treat the work as serious and important, but never take themselves too seriously and remember that schools should be filled with smiles, laughter, friendship, and collaboration. They know that the more fun they have, the more likely they will accomplish their goals. They encourage everyone in their circle to celebrate themselves and each other. In districts, schools, and classrooms staffed by effective and innovative educators, both the students and staff therein work extremely hard. They always strive to get better, encourage risk taking, promote a growth mindset rather than a fixed one, and intentionally recognize and celebrate all the good they see occurring around them. When people know that the work is important, are encouraged to believe they can do the work, and feel confident that we will not give up on them along the way, amazing things can happen!

The most positive, passionate, and productive teachers and leaders we know continue their journey on the path to excellence by adopting and exhibiting a growth mindset in all they do. Educational psychology researcher Carol Dweck explains that people with a fixed mindset believe their intelligence and talent are simply unchangeable traits. Instead of focusing on developing and growing their intelligence or talents, they spend time simply documenting these traits. They may even believe that talent or intelligence alone creates success.[1] We vehemently disagree with any such thoughts. Like Dweck, the finest educators believe that abilities can be developed through dedication and hard work—and they align their behaviors with this belief. They instill these beliefs within their students and colleagues and encourage and recognize others for "growth mindset" behaviors they observe. Such beliefs and concomitant behaviors create a love of learning and a resilience that is essential for great accomplishment, so they do whatever they can to recognize and celebrate effort-based accomplishments. The finest educators *know the way* to success themselves, *show others the way* to success, *go the way* along the path to success with the daily words they speak and actions they take; finally, they make time to *grow each day* and to find ways to grow the students and staff they serve, celebrating successes along the way.

What It Looks Like

One Day at a Time

In Ernest Hemingway's classic novel, *The Sun Also Rises*, the character Mike is asked, "How did you go bankrupt?" His response: "Two ways. Gradually, then suddenly."[2] Excellence in education happens in much the same way. When great classroom teachers look back on a school year, the students' progress and all that has been accomplished seems incredible. It can even seem like those changes happened "suddenly." The same holds true for overall school improvement. We worked with educators at one high school who, over the course of a three-year period, went from low attendance, low test scores, low staff morale, and a less-than-stellar reputation in the community, to a school that became one of the most sought after in the entire district. If we had not known better, it might have seemed a "sudden" turnaround. Of course, the opposite is true. Long-term success comes from a one-day-at-a-time insistence on continuous, focused actions aimed at getting better every day. Repeating this pattern of intentional improvement each and every subsequent day yields results that may have seemed almost impossible to imagine only a few years earlier. Excellent teachers and leaders know that the only way to achieve "sudden" success is by purposefully achieving it one day at a time and never letting an opportunity for improvement pass them by.

"Overnight success" rarely happens overnight in any walk of life, and education is no exception. Educators and schools recognized for excellence typically have a long tradition of engaging in strategic behaviors consistently over time designed to attain such excellence. They also know that "excellence" is a moving target, and that there is no finish line. Once they reach certain goals, they immediately establish new ones, never settling for "good enough." Although we have worked with many respected colleagues who insist it takes three to five years to change the culture of a school or school district, we are not convinced significant change has to take this long. However, we do know this: Regardless of how long the process of change takes, it always begins by *acting*, not deliberating. Excellent teachers and excellent school administrators do take time to deliberate, honestly identifying their current reality, as well as where they need to be in the future. Once they do so, however, they quickly move to the action phase, implementing short- and long-term goals for what must happen and when, in order to close the gap from current status to ideal state. In addition, they do not keep these goals and action steps secret; whether they are classroom teachers or school leaders, they enlist students and staff in the goals, regularly reminding them of the goals, monitoring progress toward goals, providing feedback on the progress, and adjusting the actions steps as necessary based on progress monitoring.

Regardless of how long the process of change takes, it always begins by *acting*, not deliberating.

When working with schools on the topic of sustained school and classroom improvement, Jeff often shares the story of his early long-distance running experiences. May 17, 1991 was a humbling moment for Jeff. It was on this date he discovered the sad fact that he did not have the stamina to run a single mile. A friend who was a runner invited him for a run; not thinking too much about it, he readily agreed. Even though he was very active and in fairly good shape at the time, he had not run any significant distance in many, many years. The friend wanted to run three miles and that seemed like a simple task, so off they went for a three-mile run. After just less than a mile, with chest pounding, body aching, and breathing laborious, Jeff gave up. The friend kept going while Jeff turned around and walked back, feeling just a tad humiliated. On that long, sad walk, Jeff set a goal for himself: He decided he would run a full marathon. The next day, Jeff set out for another run. He knew exactly how far he had made it the previous day, so his goal was to make it that far again and just a little bit more. In fact, he decided to run to the next furthest mailbox before stopping that day. He managed to do this and followed the exact same pattern each and every day thereafter. Each day, he would simply run the same distance as the day before, and then tack on one more mailbox. On some days, the next mailbox was literally only inches apart from the previous day's mailbox. On other days, the next mailbox was several hundred yards further. Whatever the distance, he knew he could make it the same distance covered the day before and one mailbox more. By following this regimen, he slowly, but steadily, increased his distance. It was not long before he ran his first 5K race. Not long after that, he was ready for his first 10K. He was thrilled to reach half-marathon status and then, on Thanksgiving Day 1993, he ran his first full marathon, 26.2 miles! In approximately two and a half years, he had progressed from not being able to run a single mile to running 26.2 miles. To some people who knew him, this seemed like a "sudden" accomplishment, but they, of course, did not know the daily regimen he followed to accomplish this "overnight" success.

Our improvement as individual educators as well as school and district improvement is not unlike Jeff's marathon journey. Rarely do our successes and sustained improvement occur overnight or by

accident. Instead, they occur over time and happen almost impercep-
tibly during the improvement journey itself, through targeted goal setting and intentional action steps. Indeed, if we continue pushing the
needle forward each and every day of our professional lives, it astounds
us when we look back at where we were previously and to where we
grew over time; it almost seems like it happened "suddenly." Too often,
we seek the quick fix or magic bullet when, instead, we simply need
to keep getting better—each and every minute of each and every day.
There are several parallels between Jeff's long-distance running story
and the continuous improvement journeys of educators, schools, and
districts worth considering:

- We must begin by establishing an audacious vision. Deciding
  to run 26.2 miles when one cannot currently run a single
  mile is more than a mere goal; it is a grand vision of the
  future. Educators, schools, and districts who accomplish great
  things start by establishing a far-reaching—but attainable—
  vision of a better future.

- We need to identify clear, daily steps (goals) that will move
  us toward our vision. In Jeff's running quest, he decided to
  set a daily goal for himself: to run just a little bit further than
  he had the day before. As educators, if we get just a little bit
  better on a daily basis, pretty soon we will be a whole lot
  better.

- We need the right equipment, support, and knowledge
  to help us get better. On Jeff's very first run, he began by
  lacing up his basketball shoes, which likely contributed
  to his inability to run a single mile. The very next day, he
  purchased actual running shoes and running clothes. This
  new equipment itself was not the major factor in successfully
  running a marathon, but having the proper equipment
  maximized his chances for success. In our professional

improvement, we also require the necessary materials and professional learning experiences if we are to succeed. Rarely can we get to where we are going if we do not have the right people and resources to support us.

- We must start now. Whether the vision is running a marathon, sending a man to the moon, or becoming more innovative in our instructional practices, the time to start is now. It is far better to start improving now, getting better steadily, than to wait until we think we can do something perfectly.

- We need to celebrate mini-victories along the way. When Jeff ran his first 5K race, he was on top of the world. The same thing happened after his first 10K and half-marathon. These accomplishments along his path to the larger vision kept him going. In our professional improvement journey, we must also recognize and celebrate successes along the way to the larger prize.

Excellent educators set lofty, long-term visions, as well as shorter-term goals. Then, they act—and continue moving forward. They believe in themselves, their students, and their colleagues, knowing that, together, they will eventually get there. Perhaps not always as fast as they would like and certainly not without some setbacks along the way, but in these journeys, as with Jeff's running journey, persistence defeats resistance. We will eventually reach our vision of the future if we keep making forward progress. Professional improvement, whether for an individual educator, an entire school, or a district, is never easy. As with most things in life worth pursuing, it takes a vision as well as the dedication and determination to identify which steps to take, and when to take them, in order to attain "overnight" success.

Hypocrisy . . . or Growth?

Of the traits that excellent educators share in common, perhaps none is as prevalent as a willingness to change when they learn a better way. This change can be a change in practice or a change in mindset. Both are vitally important and a distinctive characteristic of educators who *grow each day*. Excellent educators regularly reflect on their performance and periodically change their mindset and professional practices based on the results they are getting, the research they are conducting, best practices they observe elsewhere, professional literature they read, and interactions they have with fellow educators in their P²LN. Change comes to them naturally; they consider adjustments and revisions obvious and normal behavior for people in any profession—and certainly one as important as education. In fact, the finest educators consider it professional malpractice to *not* change when they learn new and better ways of doing their work.

> The finest educators consider it professional malpractice to *not* change when they learn new and better ways of doing their work.

Unfortunately, not everyone in the world—including the world of education—is as open to change and excited about changing their mindsets and practices. In fact, some educators with whom we have worked are even quite resistant to change of any kind. In most cases, this is not the result of any personality flaw or staunch insistence that they are already "good enough." Instead, it is often the result of fear. Fear about what the change will mean for them and whether they have the capacity to change. Great teachers and leaders understand this fear on the part of their colleagues (and students and parents), and work to patiently and clearly explain the process when initiating any significant change. The explanation always starts by making the case for *why* change is occurring and showing that it is not merely for the sake of change, but because there is a new and better way to fulfill the mission and accomplish the vision.

Leadership trainer John Maxwell suggests, "Change is inevitable. Growth is optional." We agree that change is inevitable. We also agree that for *some*, growth is optional. However, excellent educators do not view growth as optional. They view it as a necessary, important, and even exciting aspect of their work. To them, change creates opportunity. Although it is true that effective change agents carefully plan any change initiatives to be carried out in their classrooms or schools, communicating every step of the way and inspiring others to see the need for change, they know that some in the school community will continue to resist, and some will go so far as to openly rebel or try to sabotage change efforts. In such instances, effective change agents keep the focus on the goals ahead as well as the very best people they are serving who will benefit from the change, enlisting them in the change efforts. At the same time, they cannot always simply ignore the saboteurs among them. Although typically small in number, such naysayers can destroy improvement efforts if not held accountable.

We have worked with many terrific teachers and administrators who have shared with us the ways in which negative staff members—the "negaholics"—in their schools fight change. On more than one occasion, these amazing educators told us that they were accused of being "hypocrites" by their less effective colleagues for supporting a change in practice. One example is when we make changes to traditional grading and reporting practices. Administrators and teacher leaders who move from traditional practices—such as assigning zeros for missing work and subtracting points for various infractions not related to learning standards—to more fair, accurate, and standards-based practices, are met with cries of, "But you used to give zeros when you were teaching!" Or, "I remember you used to take ten points off for any assignment that did not have a student's name on it!" Another example we encountered recently came from a middle-school principal who happened to be a former middle-school basketball coach. The current coach at his school wanted to extend the interscholastic basketball program from a seventh- and eighth-grade program to include a sixth-grade team. The coach indicated he would be "cutting" students who tried out, keeping only twelve players on the team. The principal indicated he was not comfortable with "cutting" sixth-grade students from athletic teams, and patiently explained his rationale for this belief. The coach accused him of hypocrisy, since he knew that when the principal was a coach himself, he regularly cut students who tried out for his seventh- and eighth-grade teams.

Is it "hypocritical" to change one's mind or practices over time? Or, is it a sign of one's ongoing growth, study, learning, and reflection? We are left dumbstruck whenever we hear of educators who change their mind over time referred to as hypocrites. Imagine a doctor, mechanic, architect, or engineer who chose to continue practicing the same way over time, relying on inferior methods rather than adopting new and better techniques. We doubt they would remain in business very long. Excellent educators realize that education should be held to this same standard; when we find a new and better way of doing some aspect of our work, it becomes a moral imperative to adopt the change—regardless of how difficult the path to change will be or the level of resistance we will meet along the way. Educators who grow each day are not afraid of change, and do not back down when accused of hypocrisy for suggesting we stop doing something they did themselves earlier in their careers. In fact, they calmly state the obvious: *No, I am not a hypocrite. It is true that I, too, used to do that. However, I have grown over time. I learned a great deal. I found people in other places having greater success with a different method. I realized that my thinking on this issue was wrong, and I want to make it right. I am not a hypocrite. I want to model something important for the school community, most importantly, our students: that I am a lifelong learner who makes mistakes. Usually, I am not aware they are mistakes at the time I am making them, or I would not—obviously—be making them. However, when I do realize the error of my ways, I choose to change, rather than continuing with the mistaken approach.*

Change is inevitable for the best educators. For them, growth is not optional!

Encourage Effort; Celebrate Success

Excellent educators tend to be extremely hard-working and joyful people. Moreover, they tend to encourage both effort and joy within others as they go about teaching and leading them. Classroom teachers and school administrators also tend to be intelligent men and women. In fact, every single classroom teacher and administrator serving in a public school has earned at least one, and often, several college degrees. However, when we ask these people what has made the difference in their lives—their innate intelligence and academic degrees, or the hard work and effort they put into all that they do—the answer is invariably that effort vastly outweighs intellect. The vast majority of adults working in schools possess a level of measurable intelligence in the same general range. What separates great educators from merely good educators is not intellect, but effort and attitude. The same holds true for any group of students in a typical classroom setting. To be certain, some students with exceptional cognitive abilities exist at either end of the spectrum, but, in general, the vast majority of students possess a level of intellect similar to their classmates. Once again, the variables determining which students will surpass all expectations are effort and attitude. Excellent educators believe that successful people succeed based more on their effort than their ability. They also believe that the more joyful people are, the more likely it is that they will want to put forth the effort required to succeed. Therefore, they promote effort and a joyful attitude in everything they do.

What separates great educators from merely good educators is not intellect, but effort and attitude.

Excellent educators start the process of encouraging effort by simply sharing their own stories of success. Schools around the world are filled with educators who, when asked, can readily share a story of personal success achieved through sheer determination and effort. Savvy teachers and administrators do not wait to be asked, however; instead, they eagerly share their stories with the staff members and students they lead as authentic examples of the importance of effort. They also send consistent messages that, through ongoing effort, we can actually become smarter. They sincerely believe this to be the case and behave accordingly, by constantly learning new skills and gaining new knowledge. For some who insist "intelligence" is a static trait, consider these questions: Do you know more today about any subject than you did last year? Five years ago? Is there anything you can do today that you could not do a year ago? Five years ago? We have yet to meet the person who could honestly answer "no" to these questions. Humans are born to learn, to gain new knowledge and skills. We gain that new knowledge and skills through effort and become "smarter" as a result.

In recent years, we have seen a "Growth Mindset" bulletin board in schools across the country. You have probably seen it, too. It encourages us to change our words such as, "I'm no good at this" to "What am I missing?" Or, "This is too hard" to, "This may take some time and effort." We applaud the sentiment of such words, and educators who create such bulletin boards as a way to send powerful messages about the importance of effort over innate skills and intellect. As always, though, the variable is not the bulletin board itself; nearly all schools these days seem to have one. The variable is whether we behave in ways aligned to these words and constantly reinforce them with our students and each other. In classrooms with great teachers and schools with great principals, the focus isn't the words on the wall, but the belief and behaviors those words encourage: optimal effort every day.

Another way excellent educators promote effort is to celebrate it when they see it. They set the standard for working hard, showing grit, persevering through challenges, and putting forth focused effort through deliberate practice. After setting the standard in this way and reinforcing it regularly, they next set about finding examples of it occurring and celebrating it in any number of ways. They may avoid praising "talent" or "intelligence," but they rarely miss an opportunity to praise effort and successes realized through persistent effort.

Collectively, we have nearly 100 years of service in the education profession and have visited thousands of schools around the world during our careers. One of the most impactful things we have noticed that all great schools have in common is a joyful culture. In great schools, teachers genuinely like each other, their students, and their administrators. The same goes for the students and administrators there. Teachers believe that students will work harder for teachers who they love, and in classrooms that are fun. Likewise, administrators in joyful schools know that teachers will put forth more effort when they love their colleagues and have fun while working. Those of us in education have picked a profession that matters. As we mentioned previously, the difficult thing is it matters each and every minute of each and every day. The work can be exhausting, stressful, and, at times, frustrating. The very best educators experience these emotions just like anyone else, but they never let that frustration or stress show. They work hard and have fun daily. In fact, they believe that the harder they work, the more fun they will have. More importantly, they send these messages to the adults and students they serve, cultivating a community of learners who view hard work and fun as two sides of the same coin.

In recent years, few people have made as significant an impact in the area of promoting effort over "smarts" than Carol Dweck. She maintains that, "Emphasizing effort gives a child a variable that they can control. They come to see themselves as in control of their success."[3] Excellent teachers and leaders know that emphasizing effort— and joyfully celebrating effort-based success—apply not only to their students, but also to themselves. Emphasizing and celebrating effort is another way they grow each day.

Connect!

Students who feel more connected to their classrooms and schools tend to be more successful than students who feel disconnected from their school. Often, these feelings of "connectedness" arise from feeling connected to their teachers and fellow classmates. Excellent educators do everything in their power to "connect" their students to their classrooms and schools. We believe that our very best teachers and leaders are also people who feel more connected to the schools they serve than colleagues who feel less connected. As a result, they are often finding new ways to connect themselves, their colleagues, and their students to their own school community. In recent years, they have added a new layer and begun connecting themselves and those they serve to fellow educators and school communities across the globe. Through social media and various technology tools, educators are no longer limited to participating in learning experiences available in their immediate surroundings. With the power of social media, educators can connect with people everywhere and engage in conversations about how to make learning more authentic, relevant, and personal.

One of the most important ways excellent educators *grow each day* in today's society is by becoming a connected educator, establishing and maintaining a Personal and Professional Learning Network (P^2LN) of fellow educators. P^2LNs are an amazing opportunity to extend professional learning beyond one's immediate locale and to access anytime, anywhere, learning from a community that includes some of the most giving and forward-thinking educators we know. Our own journeys to becoming connected to our P^2LNs and experiences since then compelled us to write a book, *What Connected Educators Do Differently*,[4] in which we describe eight key characteristics of "connected" educators that set them apart and help them become better teachers and leaders. We believe that being a connected educator is a mindset more than anything else. The connected educator mindset believes that educators can leverage online communities of practice to improve their effectiveness and enhance student learning. The connected educator mindset believes that educators can and should establish networks to share practices, access experts, and solve problems. The connected educator mindset also believes that teachers and leaders are in the learning business and, therefore, also serve as lead learners, constantly reaching out to learn, share, and collaborate with a network of fellow learners who are equally passionate about learning. In short, we define "connected educators" simply as *ones who are actively and constantly seeking new people, opportunities, and resources to grow as professionals.*

Connecting with people around the world has, frankly, never been easier than it is today. In our opinion, the most prevalent and best way to get and stay connected with passionate educators willing to learn with you and support you in your efforts to grow remains the educator community active on Twitter. In fact, when speaking to groups of educators, Jimmy often makes the point that if you are not connecting outside your own school or district to learn and grow, it is simply a choice you are making at this point to not take advantage of a relatively easy way to expand your professional learning resources. By now, we

suspect that every educator serving in a school today is either connected via Twitter themselves or they know at least one colleague who
is connected to a P²LN through Twitter. Ask yourself this: Who are the
people in your schools who make the time and effort to connect with
educators around the world via Twitter? Are they the slackers in your
school? We suspect not. In fact, we would hazard a guess that connected educators in schools everywhere tend to be among the hardest-working and most passionate educators in the entire school district in which you serve. This is what makes up the Twitter educational
community: the best of best, professionals who deeply care about what
they do and the people they serve. Professionals who are willing to give
of themselves, even after a long day of work, to help someone they do
not even know by providing a resource or connecting them with someone who can help with a problem they are experiencing. Professionals
who are relentless about getting better and actively seek out others who
can help them achieve their goals.

The Twitter educational community is simply one of the most
powerful tools available to educators serving in any role at any school
to grow professionally. If you are already a connected educator, con-
gratulations on *growing each day* in this way. If you have yet to start the
journey, it is not too late. In fact, today would be an ideal time to start.
There are people out there waiting to help you on your journey; in fact,
we are so passionate about the power of the P²LN, that we invite you
to reach out to any of us via Twitter at any time if you need help getting started. Start small, perhaps by setting aside a few minutes, several
times a week to scan some tweets posted by other educators and tweet
out a few items of your own. You may want to share a resource you
have found helpful, share some pictures of engaging learning occurring in your classroom or school, or simply share a quote that inspires
you. Some days, you will find yourself on a roll of extremely worthwhile interactions and find that your few minutes turn into an hour
or more of time invested in connecting and growing. Start small and

stay the course. We suspect you will reap the benefits that thousands of other educators around the world have enjoyed by staying connected.

The Challenge Sweet Spot

"This is boring!" Unfortunately, we hear students say this fairly often. As a matter of fact, although they may not use these exact words, we often hear teachers complain that the professional learning events they are required to attend are less than exhilarating. However, excellent educators know that authentic learning is never boring. Whether we're talking about seventh-grade students or seventh-grade teachers, all human beings are innately wired to learn, and whenever we are truly learning something new, we are engaged. However, when we assign tasks to our students or our staff members that are too easy for them or when we "teach" them something that they already know, it should not evoke surprise when some respond unenthusiastically. On the other hand, if we "overchallenge" our kids or colleagues, they have every right to feel frustrated with the assigned work. Excellent educators know they need to constantly challenge their learners—whether students or adults—creating lessons, activities, and assignments designed at the "sweet spot" level of challenge, the level that is neither too hard, nor too easy. In order to get better, we all need to engage in "productive struggle," tackling challenges that are just beyond our current abilities.

Improving by engaging in challenging activities is not limited to the classroom. Many years ago, Jeff took up the game of tennis. By his own admission, he was not very good, but he did have a desire to improve. His closest friend at the time was a fellow teacher who lived nearby. They had similar schedules and a common tennis court available, so they had the opportunity to practice together frequently. Even though this person was a close friend, Jeff hated playing tennis with him; it was "boring." You see, as bad as Jeff was at the game, his friend was even worse, a step below Jeff's meager ability level. Whenever they played, Jeff would win nearly every game, without much of a challenge. Jeff realized two things: First, he was bored playing tennis against his friend. Secondly, he was not getting any better as a tennis player when playing against this friend. On the other hand, there was another person on Jeff's tennis team who was just a bit better than Jeff at tennis. Most of the times when they played, Jeff would typically lose sets by scores of 6–3 or 6–4. On rare occasions, Jeff was even able to win a set. Playing against someone of that skill level was precisely what Jeff needed to stay totally focused and engaged during every single shot of every single game. Moreover, he found himself getting better whenever he played against this person. In this instance, *winning* was not nearly as important as getting better. Although a competitive person by nature, Jeff was less worried about competing against an opponent (winning) than he was about competing against himself (improving).

Jeff's tennis experiences are worth considering when we are planning lessons and practice opportunities for students or professional learning experiences for staff. Like Jeff, most students and staff possess a sincere urge to get better and better at something that truly matters to them. However, they are not going to get any better doing something that does not challenge their current capabilities or skill sets. Effective classroom teachers and leaders planning professional learning experiences never forget this and constantly monitor the work they are assigning, asking: Are we assigning work that is too easy? Is it stuff our kids (or staff) already know and can do with no real challenge to them? If so, they may find learners losing interest in the work, possibly complying with the assignment by doing it, but without being authentically engaged. Moreover, knowing the likelihood they will grow and get better as a result of the "learning" is slim, they may disengage completely. At the same time, we cannot design lessons that are overly challenging. In our tennis analogy, if Jeff had played against Serena Williams— who presumably has the ability to defeat him 6–0 every single set—he would neither improve, nor be overly engaged in the game for long.

Great educators know it is equally important that we not assign work too far beyond our learners' current skill set.

When designing learning experiences for our students and our colleagues, we need to take into account each individual's current "Point A" and then identify each one's "Point B" on the learning continuum, challenging each to extend their learning. We must provide challenging learning experiences that stretch everyone based on their current level of proficiency. We must keep expecting educators to grow and get better by providing learning experiences that matter to them and that are challenging, yet attainable. Motivating our students—and ourselves—to embrace the work on the road to mastery require us to intentionally assign tasks and performances that push each individual just beyond their current ability level and even beyond their comfort zone. As stated earlier, one source of frustration in classrooms and during professional learning sessions is the frequent mismatch between what people must do and what people can do. When what they must do exceeds their capabilities, the result is anxiety. When what they must do falls short of their capabilities, the result is boredom. We must find the challenging "sweet spot" in between.

Educators who *grow each day* know that when they have a compelling goal that challenges them to give their best, it brings a feeling of exhilaration to their lives. They know that many of life's greatest rewards are earned when they reach just a little higher than perhaps even they believed they could. When they are challenged to grow, that is when they are in the *flow* of learning. The same holds true for the students and staff members they teach; as a result, they consistently push others by providing rigorous—but engaging—challenges. Finally, when in doubt, they err in the direction of overchallenging versus underchallenging, knowing that little is gained when we are underchallenged.

Run the Experiment. Reflect. Repeat.

The very best educators we know are not afraid to take risks. In fact, they view risk taking, learning from failure, and experimenting as critical components of their *grow-each-day* mentality. They grow by trying out new ideas, learning from their experiments, and then setting out again in a never-ending pursuit of improvement. When they have an idea for what might be a new and better way of doing something, or when they are approached by a colleague who wants to try a new way of doing something, they respond with, "Let's run the experiment." Whether the experiment is a new way to deliver instruction in a classroom, a new way to run a faculty meeting, or even a new way to manage the school cafeteria, they reflect on the process as well as the results. They determine whether the experiment was successful (students learned more, staff members were more engaged, the cafeteria became a better place in which to eat and socialize). Based on this reflection, they do one of three things:

1. Scrap the idea completely.

2. Keep the new way in place as originally designed.

3. Keep the new way in place with modifications to the original plan.

All three are viable outcomes. What seems like a good idea does not always pan out; when that is the case, great educators reflect honestly and adjust—and sometimes the adjustment is simply scrapping what they thought was going to be a good idea. However, whichever option they choose after running the experiment and then reflecting on it, the next step is to repeat the process. Excellent educators embrace change as a way to make their lives—and their students' lives—more meaningful.

Some people resist change. They are satisfied with the way things are, and if they are already getting good results, do not see the reason for change. Other people seem innately wired for constant change; they always strive for the "next best thing." Both approaches can, in fact, be risky; too much change can be as harmful as not enough change. There is such a thing as too much change, and changing merely for the sake of change is counterproductive, but in general, excellent educators tend to be more open to change—as long as they can envision a compelling "why?"

Marcie Faust is the director for innovative learning for a school district outside of Chicago. In her role, she leads change initiatives relating to teaching and learning that impact every teacher in the district. When leading such change, she starts by reminding herself that not all staff members are as excited about the change as she typically is. So rather than focusing on getting them excited, she encourages her colleagues to at least "run the experiment" and see what happens. Marcie knows that people grow more through effort—learning, and trying new things—than they do from repeating the same thing over and over again. Marcie's success in getting her colleagues to at least experiment with the status quo starts with her relationship skills. She *knows the way* and is constantly seeking out new people, resources, and research explaining new tools and practices that are working elsewhere so she can learn and know even more prior to suggesting any changes. She *goes the way* by experimenting with the change herself, trying out new ideas on a small scale to see if it is worth pursuing with the larger community. She *shows the way* by setting up demonstration classrooms, teaching, and co-teaching lessons for others to observe. Throughout the process, she is present and shows she cares about the people with whom she works by sharing her passion, energy, and positivity. She encourages others and provides the necessary support when others are willing to step out of their comfort zones. People trust her and, as a result, are more willing to take a chance.

When encouraging others to take a chance and become more innovative in their roles, Marcie shares three simple steps:

1. Start small.

2. Try something new.

3. Learn from your students.

When working with Marcie—and other effective change agents—many things are negotiable. Some, however, are not. For instance, refusing to try at all is not an option. If the possibility exists that we can do better, we must run the experiment. Having said that, the "experiment" can be a small one; starting small is an option and, typically, a wise one. Perhaps it involves trying out a single new app on an iPad as a way to teach a specific math skill. Or maybe it involves "flipping" just one faculty meeting. It could mean dramatically changing or eliminating homework—but only for one week to see what happens. Whatever we are experimenting with, we can always start small first so we can possibly go large later. Next, we are in the learning business; we must be lifelong learners. Living as a learner means trying out new ideas and new techniques. We can start small, but it must be with something new, something we have not tried before and are now merely recycling as something "new." Years ago, when technology was just making its way into schools, we knew a number of teachers and administrators who, when asked to set a professional goal for the school year, would say something along the lines of, "Get better at technology." Some even recycled this vague and random "goal" for more than one year. Thankfully, we have moved beyond this, but our professional learning goals must include trying something new, even if we are only trying it on a small scale. Finally, there is much we can—and should—learn from our students when running the experiment. This is especially true when the "something new" is related to technology. In the past five years, we have witnessed students of all ages—including kindergartners—teaching their teachers how a learning tool on an iPad works, or how to do something on an interactive whiteboard, or how some social media platform works. Great teachers are not afraid to learn from their students. Of course, we also learn from our students simply by observing them and monitoring their progress to inform us whether our efforts are producing the desired results.

Educators are in the "growing" business. In fact, when we ask teachers and administrators what they believe the purpose of school is, many use the word *growth* in their responses. However, excellent educators know that we are not only in the business of growing our students, but also ourselves. As a result, they keep an open mind when it comes to changing current practices. Whether it stems from their own ideas or the ideas of others with whom they are connected, they are always willing to "run the experiment" as a way of seeking new and better ways to do their work. They reflect on such experiments and repeat the process regularly. Knowing that constant experimentation can be overwhelming, they remind themselves to start small when trying something new. They also remember that one of their greatest learning resources are the students they serve, and enlist their students as key players in the experiment.

Surround Yourself with Excellence

Excellent educators continue to grow and get better, in part, because they surround themselves with others who are also committed to excellence. Unfortunately, almost every school we visit includes a few staff members who are negative, underperforming, or not committed to the mission, vision, values, and goals of the overall team. We have found the same holds true for administrators, too. Although the overwhelming majority of teachers and administrators are top-notch professionals whose hearts and minds are firmly planted in the right place, there are almost always a few outliers among them who seem incapable of finding the joy in what they do or in serving as part of a team that is committed to doing what is best for kids. These people may be in the minority, but the impact they have on school communities cannot be ignored. Failing to address these difficult people allows their attitudes to impede either the growth of their fellow educators or the growth of their students. Educators who *grow each day* are keenly aware of the few negative colleagues among them and commit to behaving in ways designed to lessen these colleagues' impact on themselves and other colleagues.

The best in our profession intentionally surround themselves with the best. They are comfortable with who they are and never feel threatened by others who are viewed as highly talented. Less effective people surround themselves with people who look up to them, rather than surrounding themselves with people to whom they look up. Those who are motivated by improving their personal and professional skill sets are able to accept learning from others who have different experiences, knowledge, and wisdom, regardless of their title, age, or gender. Excellent teachers deal with difficult colleagues and keep their focus on what matters most by always seeking out colleagues who are equally passionate about their profession and the students they serve. These include both colleagues within their own school setting and colleagues with whom they have connected via their P²LN. Whether at school or away from school, the best teachers surround themselves with excellence in order to keep growing. Likewise, excellent administrators are intentional about the people with whom they choose to connect, seeking out others, both locally and globally, who are interested in connecting and collaborating as a way to grow and improve.

The best in our profession intentionally surround themselves with the best.

An even more important way that school and district leaders work to surround themselves—and every staff member and student in the school—with excellence is through the hiring process. Todd has long maintained that if you have great teachers, you have a great school. So when we boil everything down to its core, there are truly only two ways to improve any school: Hire better teachers and/or improve the ones who are already in place. Knowing this, teachers and leaders who surround themselves with excellence do so, in part, as a way to help each other continually improve. Perhaps even more importantly, whenever there is a teaching position open in a great principal's school, that principal treats that opening as a precious opportunity to improve the school and, as a result, has a single, laser-like focus to hire the very best teacher, regardless of experience, race, gender, or any other variable. The only variable that does matter is that the new person be truly excellent. When great principals have a teaching opening, they invite their best teachers to take active roles in the hiring process. When Todd served as a principal, he let both the interviewing team and the candidates know the school's audacious goal for the process, which was to hire someone so great that instead of hiring someone who would become more like the current teachers, they would hire someone that the team would want to become more like in some way. When Jimmy became a principal, he took Todd's advice to heart. During the interview process, Jimmy would often ask the following question to prospective candidates: "Our goal is to hire someone so amazing that when we hire you, I'd rather the other teachers in the school become more like you than have you become more like the other teachers. Tell me something so amazing about you as a teacher that I would want every other teacher in our school to emulate."

It is our *people*, not our *programs*, that make the difference in schools.

We have said it before and will reiterate it here: It is our *people*, not our *programs*, that make the difference in schools. Since people are our most precious asset and the most important variable impacting student success, there is perhaps nothing we do that is more important than recruiting, hiring, and retaining the right people—and keeping the wrong people away. In education, we simply cannot afford to get this one wrong. In schools with great administrators and great teachers collaborating on the process, they get it right. When hiring, they worry less about technical skills, content knowledge, and experience in favor of attitude, integrity, and a growth mindset. They are also careful about the phrase "hiring for fit." Hiring for "fit" is certainly considered by some human resources experts as best practice. The danger lies in interpreting this to mean, "hiring people who are a lot like us." Instead, we should hire teachers who vary widely in their many attributes and who, in fact, complement, rather than mirror, our own skill sets. The "fit" we aim for is one who will fit in when serving in a school community focused on and committed to excellence.

Breakfast of Champions

We have all been told that breakfast is the most important meal of all; it influences every aspect of our approaching day, including how we perform physically and mentally. Unfortunately, we know a number of people who overlook the importance of breakfast, either grabbing an unhealthy snack on the go with a cup of coffee for their daily breakfast, or skipping it altogether. When asked, our non-breakfast-eating friends often say they are just too busy in the morning to set aside time for actually sitting down to eat a nutritious breakfast. We get it; our lives are incredibly hectic. In contrast to those hungry friends, we have other friends who intentionally schedule this time into their busy morning on a daily basis and still get as much (maybe more?) accomplished as their non-breakfast-eating colleagues. Feedback is just a bit like breakfast. We know it is important, so important in fact, that leadership expert Rick Tate took to calling feedback "The Breakfast of Champions." Yet, many of us fail to actively seek feedback from those we serve—including our students. Excellent teachers and school administrators know the importance of feedback as a way for them to grow and improve. They may occasionally miss breakfast, but they never miss an opportunity to ask others how they are doing.

Truthful, timely feedback can have a powerfully positive impact on people. We all want to know how well we are doing, whether that comes in the form of praise for a job well done, coaching to improve performance, or even redirection when necessary. We firmly believe that providing and receiving clear feedback on a regular basis is not only an excellent strategy for improving performance, but also for instilling a sense of pride and satisfaction among those receiving the feedback. Feedback can be done quickly, it costs nothing, and it can turn performance around fast. In education, the term *feedback* has gained quite a bit of attention recently, due in part to the work of John Hattie and his book *Visible Learning*.[5] In Hattie's meta-analysis identifying more than a hundred variables influencing student performance, feedback comes in at number ten on the list and is consistently shown to have a high impact on achievement. Interestingly, Hattie shares that he was mistaken in how he originally defined feedback, thinking it was something teachers provided students. In fact, the most powerful feedback occurs when students let teachers know how they are doing. Obviously, excellent teachers actively and regularly seek feedback from students about their learning (e.g., finding out what they know, where they are having misunderstandings, and when they are disengaged). However, great teachers also seek feedback from their students about how, as teachers, they are doing in their job. Such teachers sincerely value student input and want to learn what students like about the class and the instruction, what they dislike about it, what could be better about the class, and what they think works well and not so well. It can be scary asking our students how we are doing; most of us do not enjoy receiving negative feedback. However, the finest teachers use all feedback—both the positive and the more critical—as an important component of their own growth plan.

Rather than leaving this growth opportunity to chance, excellent administrators are equally persistent about regularly seeking feedback. Such school and district administrators we know have systems in place for periodically eliciting specific feedback about their job performance. Even the best leaders in the business know they will always get at least one or two comments that are unfairly critical. Criticism is almost inevitable, and great leaders seem to possess an internal radar letting them know when they can legitimately ignore these unfair comments. These same leaders welcome and even embrace honest, specific, critical feedback. They relish this feedback even more than positive feedback, knowing that this kind of input can help them grow and improve.

Regular feedback—much like breakfast— is a healthy way to grow.

Whether seeking feedback from our students about their progress or each other about our own progress, we are really asking for information focused on three key feedback questions:

1. Where are we/they going? (sometimes referred to as "Feed Up")

2. How are we/they going? (sometimes referred to simply as "Feed Back")

3. Where to next? (sometimes referred to as "Feed Forward")

Excellent educators regularly ask for feedback as a means of better understanding if they are moving in the right direction, if they are acting effectively, and where others think they need to go next to get better. They look forward to regular feedback—much like breakfast—as a healthy way for them to grow.

TEACH 4, LEAD 4, LEARN 4

Teachers and leaders who stand out as excellent exhibit a clear pattern of growing each day professionally and personally. They know that significant improvement over time stems from a commitment to get just a little bit better every day. They do not apologize for changing their minds when they learn of new and better ways to do their work, because they know that change is part of growth and a sign of learning. Realizing that the root of most success is intentional work and effort, they encourage effort-based growth in themselves and others, and celebrate successes related to effort. These educators know that if they are to become the very best they can be, it is not enough to connect solely with the people in their immediate surroundings; they look both inside their own school or district and also around the globe for new people, opportunities, and resources that will help them get better. They challenge themselves and the students and staff they serve with tasks that are attainable, but that also push them to extend themselves beyond what even they may think is possible at first. They are always willing to experiment and take chances if it means they can learn new and better ways of fulfilling their professional mission. They surround themselves with excellence in everything they do and are not afraid of seeking support from others who may know more than they do. Finally, they are intentional about seeking feedback, and especially seek critical feedback that will help them grow.

Teach 4

Here are four educators we believe stand out as exemplars for *Growing Each Day*:

1. Andrea Trudeau (@Andrea_Trudeau) is a National Board Certified Teacher who has taught both language arts and social studies at the middle-grades level. She is currently serving as a librarian information specialist at Shepard Middle School in Illinois. In both roles, Andrea has been a leader of the *run the experiment mindset* and is always willing to try out new ways to enhance teaching and learning.

"Trust my crazy" isn't something that many people expect to hear from a library information specialist. We are traditionally thought of as "shushing" types, buried in books in a world revolving around the Dewey Decimal System. In other words, we are supposed to keep it neat and play it safe. However, the reality is I would not excel in or enjoy my role as a library information specialist today without breaking free of this stereotype and taking risks. Risks push me out of my comfort zone into a place of uncertainty, but also into a world of creativity, imagination, and excitement. They have brought lively, engaging, and often messy experiences into my school's learning commons—Maker Mondays, Breakout EDU, and the Cardboard Challenge. Risks encourage me to seek out the dreamers among the staff I work with and share new ideas that challenge their thinking and their instructional practices in order to take students to new heights. As a result of this risk taking and the vulnerability that inevitably accompanies it, students now experience the diversity and beauty of the world around us using 3D virtual reality tools and learn valuable STEM skills using droids and drones—lessons that require careful planning, preparation, reflection, and even a bit of blind faith, at times, to orchestrate. Risks continue to illuminate pathways I never knew existed before, helping me build stronger relationships with my colleagues and students, empowering me to seek out even more challenges to enhance students' learning experiences and break free from the traditional librarian stereotype. Ultimately, I have discovered that as frightening as risk taking may seem at first, the greater risk is maintaining the status quo.

2. Starr Sackstein (@mssackstein) is a Nationally Board Certified English teacher who works as a Teacher Center teacher at Long Island City High School in New York. She is the author of several books on topics ranging from alternative assessment and reflection to questioning and teaching peer feedback. Starr knows that *effective feedback* is the breakfast of champions when it comes to helping students grow and improve.

For more than a decade, I've worked with high-school students, and the single most powerful part of pushing them toward greater achievement has been around feedback. In all of the learning we do, students receive feedback in a multitude of ways: one-to-one conferences, from peers in small groups, via in-person meetings and through technology (like Voxer or Google Docs). These interactions allow students to know where they are in relation to meeting or exceeding standards, and where and how they can improve in other places. It's not enough to tell a student he is doing something well unless we can articulate the specifics of it. Reflection helps to tailor feedback effectively, offering me the perfect opportunity to listen to what kids feel they were doing well and what they struggled with. In this way, when I prefaced reading student work with their reflections, I was better able to provide specific feedback to the areas they spoke of. By simply reading these short reflective pieces first, I had a better lens to improve each student's learning and a better means of improving the way I taught mini-lessons after gathering data from the whole class. After all, feedback is a two-way street, and when kids tell us something directly or indirectly, we must adjust accordingly.

3. Paul Solarz (@PaulSolarz) is a fifth-grade teacher in Arlington Heights, Illinois, and author of the bestselling book, *Learn Like a PIRATE*. In Paul's classroom, students lead the learning in many different ways. Although students have a great deal of responsibility and ownership of their own learning, Paul knows the importance of *encouraging effort and celebrating success* to ensure they remain on track and continue to grow.

In our fifth-grade classroom, we're all about trying to become the best ME we can be. Along the way, we work hard at helping each other grow as well, because it's no fun to step on others to get to the top! Instead, we bring our peers along on our learning journey so everyone can feel successful and improve their skills. In our class-room, we don't focus on perfection or mastery; instead, we focus on gradual improvements over time based on feedback we get from our teachers and peers. Our perpetual goal is to grow, improve, and learn from our mistakes so that we're a stronger ME today than we were yesterday. This type of growth mindset requires a great deal of reflection, self-assessment, and effort in order to be successful, so teaching these three skills is vital to an improvement-focused class-room. I teach my students that not everything we put a strong effort into automatically leads to success, but that sustained effort, a keen focus, and the desire to improve are required in order to grow. My students really start to get it when I show them examples of famous people who have had to work hard for their success. Even though many of them may have been born with natural ability, they worked hard throughout their career to continue to improve, to adapt to new challenges, and to get better each day. There are thousands of stories of people who were born with amazing gifts, only to have them wasted due to a poor work ethic and little drive to improve. Therefore, we celebrate our individual goals that we achieve on a regular basis. We have a ten-minute period where I read students' sticky notes that they put on our "Goals Accomplished" board, and we congratulate each other on our accomplishments. Every child should be taught to identify their small improvements that have happened due to a strong work ethic and the drive to get better! And every child (who wants to be) should be acknowledged and celebrated for their hard work and perceived achievements. There are no rubrics required to put a note on the Goals Accomplished board in our class—students decide what achievements they're most proud of on their own! It's so important to promote strong effort in the classroom and then celebrate each of those achievements. We all need a little praise for our efforts!

4. **Cindy Kube (@cindyqb)** is a biology teacher at Salem High School in Virginia Beach, Virginia. She has taught middle- and high-school science for sixteen years. Cindy knows that her students will push themselves if they know that she believes in their ability. When assigning work to her students, Cindy strives to find the *challenge sweet spot*, designing tasks that are neither too easy, nor too difficult. When in doubt, she always errs on the side of challenging her students beyond what they think they can do, knowing that, with her support, they will rise to the challenge.

I challenge my high-school students to view the world and learning with a sense of wonder and awe. I believe that this mindset supports deeper learning by allowing students to reach higher than they thought possible; it encourages risk taking and reduces fear of failure, so that all students can engage in meaningful, relevant work that pushes the boundaries of their knowledge and understanding. As students feel confident that they can grow their abilities through challenging work, they discover a source of intrinsic motivation and the joy of lifelong learning.

As a science teacher, I have discovered that the most challenging assignments are those that provide student choice and student voice. Performance-based tasks nurture the spirit of inquiry and offer students choice in both process and product. When students are able to personalize their learning in this way, they become engaged in the intellectual stretch—the development of higher-order thinking skills. Recently, my students were asked to assume the role of a scientist at a local university, and were invited to present their research in the form of an infographic. Students chose content related to cells and made a connection with a topic such as disease, nutrition, biotechnology, or athletic endurance. As the students developed their own research questions, their sense of wonder was clearly evident in their quest for understanding and in their personal connection to their chosen topic. In my teaching practice, I focus on developing each student's ability to achieve deeper levels of understanding. I continually emphasize these skills as students grapple with content and new ideas. I support my students with intentional instruction, quality feedback that recognizes effort, and multiple opportunities for student reflection. Other strategies used to scaffold challenging work include journaling, mind mapping, and social media platforms for discussion. Although I always want my students to succeed, I also want to ensure that I am stretching them just a bit by providing challenging assignments designed to push them outside their comfort zones—that is where real learning happens!

Lead 4

Here are four educators currently serving primarily in educational leadership roles. We believe they stand out as exemplars for *Growing Each Day*:

1. **Heidi Veal (@VealHeidi)** is a champion for kids, serving as an assistant principal at an early childhood campus. She is also a presenter, blogger, co-founder and co-host of #ECEchat and #LeadUpTeach, and serves as an organizer for #EdCampDallas. Heidi is constantly on the lookout for new opportunities to grow professionally, because she knows that significant growth over time starts with *growing one day at a time.*

When it comes to growth, educators cannot be asleep at the wheel. We need to be on the lookout for ongoing growth opportunities whenever they may arise, take advantage of such opportunities, and make sure we learn something new every day. My personal motto about growth is, "The time is always right for growth!" The truth is, I cannot rely on others to make me grow, or know what I specifically need. As an empowered educator and assistant principal, I take personal ownership of my professional learning. The individualized growth I pursue on my own has, time and time again, led to exciting and unique learning experiences, not just for myself, but also for my colleagues and students in my school. For example, attending an edcamp on my own is one thing, but going together with a group from my campus extends the learning beyond the event and brings it back to our students immediately.

An essential component to being a self-fed learner is my daily connection to and with my PLN. My PLN is a constant source of inspiration and growth that, the majority of times, surpasses anything I learned in grad school. I model the value of being a connected educator routinely and encourage the teachers at my school to "find their tribe" and connect via Twitter with educators to learn, collaborate, and grow together. This was a big part of the inspiration that led my colleague, Nancy Alvarez, and I to co-found #ECEchat, a weekly Twitter chat and PLN for all early childhood educators. It is very rewarding to witness the teachers at our school beginning to build their PLN and connect with other passionate early childhood educators via #ECEchat.

A final key component of my individual growth is keeping my mind and calendar open for unique connections, opportunities, and development experiences that come my way. Thanks to Bethany Hill, a #LeadUpChat tribe-mate, I learned about the "What Great Educators Do Differently" conferences and was able to attend one with my principal and co-assistant principal. It proved to be one of the best educational conferences I have ever attended. Being alive means growing. If I'm not growing, I'm not fully living! In other words, "The time is always right for growth!"

2. Barry Saide (@Barrykid1) is a supervisor of curriculum and instruction in New Jersey. Prior to his current role, Barry served as a classroom teacher for fifteen years. In both his teaching and administrative roles, Barry has been passionate about expanding his P²LN as a way to grow each day. Barry knows that the more he is able to *connect* with other passionate educators, the more likely it is he will grow himself and the staff and students he serves.

> *For me, growing every day is the most essential part of our field. It's what I need to do because I want to model lifelong learning for our staff, students, and stakeholders. I also enjoy it. Learning is fun, and part of the growth process is feeling vulnerable. Without being attuned to what makes you vulnerable—and moving fearlessly through it anyway—we're living our educational lives at a standstill. Connecting with others every day means I need to face the venerable truth about vulnerability: I'm going to put myself out there on a personal and professional level, and others may not appreciate me. They may not even like me. And as Kid President says, "It will hurt, man!" However, if I am going to learn from and with others, I need to model an open mind, which means an open soul. So, I daily share the educational and personal knowledge I have from my fifteen years as a classroom teacher and my current role as supervisor of curriculum and instruction. Sometimes my sharing is merely connecting one person with another. I know what I don't know, and I supplement this by knowing people who do know. People are our best resources, and we are our own greatest resource when we connect people with one another.*
>
> *Connecting to others is a personal investment in ourselves and others where we may never see the benefits. I often make the parallel to teaching: As an elementary-school teacher, very often I laid*

the foundation for lifelong student learning without seeing the final result. However, I know I made a difference during every interaction with each student I served each school year as a classroom teacher. I know I've done the same with adult learners. Without connecting with others on a daily basis through face-to-face interaction and social media, I don't think I would have continued in our field. So much of living and learning is social, and that means authentically connecting with others: laughing with them, sharing a meal, providing a thought partner, or even just being a listener. My relationships with other educators inspire me to continually grow as a person and professional. I hope they do for you, too. If not, come find me and we'll grow together!

3. **Sanée Bell (@SaneeBell)** is a middle-grades principal in Katy, Texas. She is also a blogger and presenter. Sanée is passionate about students, teachers, leadership, and community. Sanée knows that nothing is more important than the people in her school who interact with the students, so she purposely *surrounds herself with excellence* so that her students are surrounded with excellence as well.

My personal growth mantra is, "Be excellent on purpose." Having this as my guiding statement helps me focus my attention and effort on the activities I participate in and the people with whom I surround myself. In order to grow professionally and personally, I make it a priority to be connected locally and globally. I establish relationships with teachers and principals who work in my district or in surrounding areas. These face-to-face connections serve as a professional safety net and sounding board for me. Wireless relationships, which are relationships created through the use of social media and other communication tools, have allowed me to extend my connections in many ways. Surrounding myself with other educators who will challenge my thinking and assumptions, who are committed to helping me think critically about instructional issues and leadership challenges, and who will give me honest feedback, are critical members of my personal and professional learning network. Growing myself as a leader is a responsibility that I refuse to give away to others. I am in charge of my personal and professional growth. The role of a principal can be a lonely seat—but only if I allow it to be.

I consider it my primary responsibility to hire well and to build the professional capital of those who are working under my leadership. It is important to me that I help others grow professionally. To do this, I collaborate with teachers to establish focus areas for professional growth. I give them written and verbal feedback on the identified growth areas, and I provide authentic, professional, personalized learning experiences that target their needs. I also provide a structure within the building that allows teachers to learn from one another. Through the implementation of the instructional-rounds process, teachers engage in classroom visits around a targeted problem of practice. Personal reflection after the rounds process is critical. It is during this process when growth, both individually and collectively, begins take place and conversations are transformed.

Excellence is only able to grow in schools if the conditions for excellence have been established, communicated, protected, and sustained. Will Durant summarized Aristotle's teaching with the famous quote, "We are what we repeatedly do. Excellence, then, is not an act, but a habit."[6] Habits are formed through intentional, reflective practice; therefore, being excellent on purpose is a personal and professional commitment to pursue excellence for myself as leader and to support others on their journey.

4. Dennis Schug (@schug_dennis) is a middle-school principal in Long Island, New York and co-founder of EdcampLI and EdcampLdrNY. He is also the co-moderator of #NYedchat. Prior to becoming a school administrator, Dennis served as a classroom teacher. During his career,

Dennis has changed his mind about many educational practices, viewing this as standard practice for lifelong learners like himself. Dennis knows the importance of asking whether it is hypocrisy or growth when we do things differently today than we did in the past.

As a teacher in the twentieth century, I felt that faculty meetings just didn't matter. They were commonly viewed as contractual obligations that interrupted the flow of a teacher's ability to get things done. Information was delivered in canned presentations, in a lecture, and, occasionally, with handouts. Topics were "covered" and generally involved federal or state mandates as well as lofty, disconnected initiatives, and miscellaneous housekeeping items. Binders, packets, and photocopies were handed out. There was no lead-up and there was rarely any follow-up, individually or in groups. And within forty-five minutes, it was over, only to happen again nine more times during the school year. In a decade of teaching, I never once remembered a meeting that positively or negatively impacted my instructional practices or my ability to grow as a teacher leader. And looking around, I could see I wasn't alone. My otherwise professional colleagues and I graded papers, read the newspaper, or made small talk just below the principal's voice.

As a school leader in the twenty-first century, faculty meetings matter. Yes, they remain a contractual obligation that must occur ten times a year, but today they center on the idea of quality time together. Simple information that must be shared is delivered in the form of a memo, email, phone call, or conversation before or after the meeting; we no longer waste valuable face-to-face time with items that can be shared more efficiently and effectively in other ways. Faculty meetings are participatory, feature protocols, and uncover strategies that model high-impact instructional practices that can be replicated in classrooms. Faculty meetings are opportunities for open dialogue about why we do what we do, and how as educators we can do better.

Rather than answers being delivered by one person who is stand-ing at the front of the room, many questions drive small-group and collaborative conversations. Dialogue is encouraged in a loop of peer instructional coaching and ongoing reflective practice. Conditions are created and driven by norms on certain expectations for one another and ourselves. Faculty meetings are now spaces and places for us to forge personal-professional relationships and foster rele-vant dialogue that promotes sharing ways in which great teachers promote a balanced culture of academic rigor and developmental responsiveness. The dialogue that either begins or continues during faculty meetings has become an important component of the flow of everyday conversational norms in our school—a learning organiza-tion. Yes, I now firmly believe that faculty meetings matter, when, as a teacher, I somewhat sheepishly admit that I did not think they mattered. When someone who worked with me then reminds me of my stance at that time, I acknowledge the reality, but also point out the current reality. I did not change my mind about faculty meetings simply because I became a principal. I changed my mind because I learned better ways of facilitating faculty meetings. Much of my learning, in fact, came from my own less-than-positive experiences as a teacher in faculty meetings and from listening to teachers serv-ing in our school. As educators, we must change our practices—and our mindsets—when we learn better techniques and ideas.

Learn 4

Here are four resources/tools/action steps you can use to further develop yourself and others relating to the standard we call *Growing Each Day*:

1. **Attend an edcamp professional learning event.** Edcamp is not a traditional professional learning conference. It is an "unconference," designed specifically for the needs of the educators attending the event.

Unlike traditional conferences, which have schedules set months in advance by the people running the conference, edcamp has an agenda that is created by the participants at the start of the event. Edcamps typically take place on Saturdays, are free to any educator, and include free breakfast and lunch. The edcamp movement has grown to the point that there is an edcamp event occurring somewhere around the globe virtually every Saturday of the year. Learn more about the edcamp professional learning experience, including past and upcoming edcamps, at edcamps.org and edcamp.wikispaces.com.

2. Participate in a Twitter chat. Twitter chats are online conversations happening seven days a week on a variety of topics. These chats are typically one hour in length and include a series of questions posed by the moderators, which initiate a professional discourse among the participants. Whether you are a first-grade teacher, a high-school biology teacher, or an administrator passionate about standards-based learning, there is a weekly Twitter chat for you. Scan the QR code to see a list of currently scheduled Twitter chats that occur weekly. Find one that feeds your area of interest and join in the conversation, connecting with other passionate educators along the way.

Schedule of Education Chats on Twitter

3. Test your growth mindset. *Mindsetonline.com* offers a quick and easy quiz designed to measure the extent to which you possess either a fixed or growth mindset. Use your results to set a goal for yourself to expand your growth mindset. Share this assessment, as well as your own results, with the students or staff you serve and invite them to increase their own growth mindset.

Test Your Mindset

4. Document growth every day, one second at a time. Watch the "One Second Every Day" TED talk by Cesar Kuriyama,[7] the person responsible for creating the app known as *1 Second Everyday.* In his presentation, Kuriyama explains how this clever idea came to be, and how it helps him grow each day. We encourage you to use the app to record a small portion of your professional life every day of the year, whether your role has you working more directly with students or adults. Do this for a year and you will be amazed when you look back at how much everyone grew from the first day of school to the last!

One Second Every
Day TED Talk

BEHAVIORS TO BELIEFS
AND BACK AGAIN

Do the best you can until you know better. Then, when you know better, do better.
—Maya Angelou

Our purpose in writing this book was to identify and describe the unique behaviors and characteristics we have observed firsthand among excellent educators serving in a variety of roles around the globe. We realize that the very word "excellence" that we focus on throughout the book is tossed around rather capriciously at times and is possibly even in danger of becoming yet another educational buzzword. That said, we believe that the specific behaviors described in the preceding pages of this book are actually aligned with standards of excellence that our very best educators set for themselves—and for the students and colleagues they serve. A quick search of the term on Google just now tells us that excellence is "... a talent or quality which is unusually good and surpasses ordinary standards .... Excellence is a continuously moving target that can be pursued through actions of integrity, being a frontrunner in services provided...meeting all obligations and continually learning and improving in all spheres to pursue the moving target."[1]

A few of these words and phrases are particularly apt when studying teachers and educational leaders. First, truly excellent educators "surpass ordinary standards." This component of *excellence* is most closely aligned to the behavior we call *Know the Way*. The education profession is a unique and special calling; nearly all who enter and remain in the field are committed to the work, and close to 100 percent of them meet the expectations set for them as laid out in any job description or evaluation process. We would be less than truthful, however, if we claimed that some educators are not better than others. The very best among us consistently go the extra mile, moving beyond what is expected and into the extraordinary. They never forget the *why* of what they do; they know their purpose and know how to fulfill it. In these pages, we strove to identify what extraordinary looks like. We wanted to both praise those who have inspired us with their excellence and to outline a path for those on the journey from ordinary to excellence.

Excellence is a "continuously moving target." Part of what sets apart the educators we described in this book from others is their acceptance that there is no finish line. The moving target of excellence requires the behavior we call *Show the Way*. Excellent educators are always on the lookout for where to go next; they possess a clear vision of the future, anticipating and reacting to changes as they move along the path forward. They never settle or rest on past accomplishments.

Finally, excellence can be pursued through "actions of integrity" and "continually learning and improving in all spheres." Such actions of integrity are most closely aligned with the behavior we call *Go the Way*, in which we find excellent educators modeling for others the behaviors they know are central to success, and which they hope to inspire others to adopt. They make time to identify shared values among the students and staff with whom they work, remind others of these values frequently, and hold everyone—most importantly, themselves—accountable for adhering to them.

Meanwhile, excellent teachers and leaders we know who can be described as "continually learning and improving in all spheres" are living out the behavior we call *Grow Each Day*. They are relentless in their pursuit of ongoing, continuous improvement for themselves. They are equally relentless in their pursuit of helping those they teach and lead get better each and every day as well.

Excellent educators, then, are those who *Know the Way, Show the Way, Go the Way*, and *Grow Each Day*. They live out these behaviors on a daily basis, realizing that all they can do today—as Angelou alludes to in the quote at this chapter's opening—is the very best they can do that day. They may not know what tomorrow will bring in terms of new and better ways of doing their work, but you can rest assured that when they learn a better way, they will do their work in a better way. In the meantime, they live each day to its fullest, allowing their guiding overall principles of *Knowing, Showing, Going*, and *Growing* to drive them to excellence.

BEHAVIORS INFLUENCE BELIEFS; BELIEFS INFLUENCE BEHAVIORS

In this book, we focused on four overarching behaviors of excellence and, within each one, we described eight specific components aligned to the behavior. The specific behaviors we describe in each chapter are actions of intention we have consistently observed among outstanding educators around the world. Oftentimes, these behaviors arise from a belief system to which these educators adhere. For example, because they believe that the better they know their students, the more likely it is their students will perform at high levels, they behave in ways designed to learn as much as they can about each student. Or, because they believe lifelong learning is important, they intentionally seek out new learning experiences throughout the school year, year after year. There are other times, however, when beliefs arise from behaviors. This may occur when a teacher or administrator is uncertain about what to believe but is either willing, or directed, to take a certain action. For example, a new teacher may be unsure of her beliefs regarding observing colleagues teach or having colleagues observe her while teaching. The school leader may encourage or even mandate peer observations. Once the new teacher is committed to the behavior (observing a colleague and allowing a colleague to observe her)—regardless of her enthusiasm about it—the teacher then begins to adopt certain beliefs about the behavior. Our hope is that if we engage teachers and administrators in behaviors we think are good for students and for the school, once they do so, they will more likely believe in the behaviors and will more likely behave in that way voluntarily moving forward.

Ideally, everyone in the school community shares the same beliefs on issues such as best teaching practices, how we treat kids, parents, and each other, and to what extent we collaborate as a team of professional educators. However, there are usually a few staff members whose past negative experiences, or simple fear of the unknown, cause them to resist change. When change is necessary and everyone has had a chance to express their opinion, the will of the majority is evident. It is then time to focus on behaviors rather than beliefs, expecting all staff members to carry out values identified as central to fulfilling the mission and achieving the vision of the overall community. In such instances, beliefs are not as important as actions, and after behaving in ways aligned with the new methods or ideas, their beliefs will hopefully come around as well. Excellent principals convince teachers to change, and excellent teachers persuade students to change—sometimes by persuading them to change their beliefs in the hopes that by believing differently they will behave differently, and for the better. At other times, they effect change, not by persuading others to change their beliefs, but by getting them to change their behaviors. Excellent educators do not waste their time or energy trying to persuade everyone in their school or classroom that a new way will be better than the old way. They certainly make the case for the new way, but they move forward. They realize that some will enlist in the journey simply because they believe in it, while others may not believe in it now but may change their beliefs once they see the results their behaviors produce.

Should I? vs. How Will I?

When Jimmy was a young educator with a growing family, he sometimes found it hard to make ends meet and certainly did not see how he could actually save any money. His salary at the time seemed to him barely enough to support himself, let alone his wife and their three young children. A teacher at his school with a similar family and income situation at the time told him something surprising: He was able to put away thousands of dollars each year into a savings account that he never touched for any reason. Jimmy wondered how this person was able to save so much more than he did. Around this same time, Jeff was teaching high school in Georgia. On some Sundays, he would attend church with his family; on other Sundays, they decided to sleep in or play golf instead. After Christmas Eve services one year, Jeff struck up a conversation with a fellow church member who was also a teacher. The teacher mentioned that he and his family had been to church services every Sunday throughout that entire year. Jeff thought this was an admirable accomplishment and wondered how his colleague managed to do this. Meanwhile, Todd was starting to speak around the world, sometimes traveling to more than one hundred speaking engagements in a single year. Always a bit of a runner, Todd would run on most days when he was home, but only occasionally when on the road. One day, when he was at a conference, another friend presenting at the conference mentioned during his keynote that he ran three miles every single morning, regardless of where he was around the world on any given day. Knowing this person's grueling travel schedule, Todd marveled that he managed to run every single morning. In each instance, the three of us wondered how these people we admired managed to do what they did so consistently. As it turns out, each of them shared a similar story, a story that hinged on the subtle, but significant, difference between asking, "Should I...?" versus asking, "How will I...?" In all three examples, the person indicated they simply committed to doing the behavior in question. Once they committed to doing the behavior, they reminded themselves daily of their commitment and when obstacles arose threatening their ability to save money, attend church services, or go for an early morning run, they steadfastly asked themselves how they were going to accomplish their goal in spite of any obstacles facing them. Jeff's friend explained that for many years, he and his wife would wake up on Sunday morning and then decide whether they would attend services that day. Eventually, they decided that it was important to them, and they simply committed to getting up and going to church every Sunday. "It's just what we do," this person said when asked about it again recently. "We no longer think about it or debate it; we are simply a family that goes to church every Sunday. You might say it has become a habit of ours." Todd and Jimmy's friends shared similar sentiments. Saving money was a non-negotiable for Jimmy's friend, and running was a daily habit for Todd's friend. Neither asked *whether* they should save money that month or go for a run that day. One committed to the habit of monthly savings and the other committed to the habit of daily running. These behaviors just became things each *did*.

Excellence, in any area, is a habit—a way of living. As in the personal examples shared above, excellent educators have become the way they are by repeatedly doing what it is they started doing on their path to excellence. They stop questioning whether they will do something they know they should do; they are already committed to doing it before they even leave for school each day. They have moved from asking, "Should I..." to challenging themselves with, "How will I...?" Whether the day's specific goal is finally reaching a reluctant learner in their classroom, attending a Saturday edcamp an hour away, or writing personal, handwritten notes to colleagues who have gone the extra mile on behalf of a student, they start not by asking *whether* they will accomplish it, but by determining *how they will* accomplish it.

Excellence, in any area, is a habit— a way of living.

Another great thing about such superstar educators is that they are also influencers, people who are respected and looked up to by their colleagues and students. Because of the success they have and the humility they exhibit in achieving success, people with whom they interact are more inclined to follow their lead. When our most respected educators treat students with dignity and respect ten days out of ten, that is a good thing. When they influence their colleagues to do the same—through their actions, rather than their words, that is a great thing. Jimmy began saving money, Jeff attended church services more regularly, and Todd became a daily runner partly because each was influenced by a colleague they knew and respected. We believe that excellence in the schoolhouse is contagious, and that is another reason we wrote this book. The more we can identify bright spots in our schools—specific behaviors that are contributing to success—and then replicate these behaviors throughout the school community, the greater our chances of changing lives for the better.

Happiness in the Daily Doing

In many schools we visit, teachers make a big deal about students' birthdays and principals have creative rituals in place for celebrating staff birthdays. We are all for celebrations in schools for any number of reasons; the work is rewarding, but very challenging and quite stressful. Like many of our colleagues, we typically embrace the notion of celebrating student and staff birthdays. We do have one administrator friend, however, who is somewhat of a curmudgeon on the topic of birthdays. In fact, when anyone wishes him a hearty "Happy birthday!" on his special day, he typically responds with: "What did I accomplish? I lived another year? Big deal." Although we happen to find the joy in birthday celebrations for people of all ages, we also tend to agree that any single day in the year is not much of a big deal at all; instead, it is the other 364 days leading up to it—when looked at collectively—that can actually amount to a pretty big deal. During the course of a long school year, the little, daily wins are easy to miss. Sometimes, it is not until the end of the school year, when we look back on where we got to and remind ourselves where we once were, that we realize all that has been accomplished over that time span. Excellent educators never lose sight of the big picture, but they also find happiness in doing their tasks daily, a few of which are exciting, and many of which are rather mundane. They may not always see daily results, but they stay the course of *knowing*, *showing*, and *going* the way while *growing each day* as well. They know that by doing so, they are making progress toward their ultimate vision with each passing day.

John Wooden, perhaps the greatest basketball coach in the history of the game, was fond of saying that little things make big things happen. In a way, "little" days make "big" ones happen, too. Birthdays are fun and worth recognizing. Graduation ceremonies are among our favorite events in the entire school year. Being recognized individually as Teacher of the Year or collectively as a National Blue Ribbon School are happy days indeed. Yet, the daily joys that occur during the other 179 or so days of teaching and learning are every bit—if not more—impressive and worthy of recognition. Excellent educators everywhere attack their daily to-do lists with determination, energy, and joy. They are remarkably upbeat, optimistic people whose cheery demeanors positively impact students and staff in their presence. They are not superhuman beings, but they do possess a superpower: the ability to teach and lead themselves and others, minute by minute, day by day, while exuding an infectious joy in the daily doing.

Seeing Possibilities, Not Problems

Excellent educators are highly competent individuals who know what to do—and then do it. They also show others what to do and how to do it, explaining why it matters, inspiring others to share in the vision, and supporting them along the way so that success is attainable for all, not just a few. They go the way they want others to go, modeling the words, actions, and values they know are important to individual as well as collective success. Finally, they grow each day, always striving for self-improvement and seeking to improve those around them. They do the best they can every single day of the year and do better when they learn how.

Knowing the way includes knowing what this profession's best practices are. Obviously, excellent educators know and implement best practices in their classrooms and their schools. They also realize that best practices evolve over time. What may be a best practice right now may well be looked at with scorn many years hence. But today, they move forward, doing the very best they can, armed with the very best knowledge they have available to them. All the while, they remain open to changing when they discover a better way. Excellence demands that we not continue doing things if the only reason we have for doing them is the fact that we have always done them. In Jeff's first year of teaching, the principal paddled children who misbehaved—and the vast majority of the staff supported and even encouraged this behavior—solely because it had always been done. There simply was no other defensible reason for doing this. Although this may seem like an extreme example, believe it or not, in every school we visit, some staff members still do things today for no other reason than because they have always done those things. Like Jeff's first principal, the people doing these things are neither bad people nor lazy professionals. In fact, many are passionate individuals dedicated to their kids, colleagues, and schools. But the truth is, some traditions in schools today serve no real learning purpose. When we notice this happening, we should confront it, discussing it openly among all affected parties. Ultimately, if we cannot support our current practice or policy in ways other than, "Well, we've always done it that way," we should seriously reconsider such practices or policies.

Excellence also requires that we be vigilant about monitoring all we do, measuring whether it is producing the desired results, and implementing new and better ideas whenever we discover them. The vast majority of educators do the very best they know how every day. Still, we must be open to the possibility that what we are doing today as "best practice" may not be the best we can do tomorrow. Doing our very best on a daily basis—and then, as Angelou challenges us, doing even better when we know better—is a way of life for professional educators of excellence. Excellent educators see possibilities where others see problems. Our profession's primary customers—the children who attend our schools—are simply too important to allow ourselves to settle for less than the very best we can provide. Moreover, they need us to see the possibilities within them, not the problems they face along the way.

Serving as an educator in today's schools can be tough. The hours are long, the pay is often substandard, the frustrations are many, and the responsibilities feel overwhelming. It might be tempting to settle for less than our very best every now and again, but excellent teachers and administrators never do. Instead, they always ask, "What is best for kids?" when approaching each day and making any decision. They never waver from this as the gold standard for decision making in their classrooms and schools. All educators get discouraged from time to time and occasionally grow weary. Excellent educators guard against this as best they can, knowing that it is when they are discouraged that they start seeing problems rather than possibilities. They start talking about the way things are, rather than the way things can become. As difficult as it may be to stay the *know-show-go-grow* course, excellent educators do not allow themselves to become weary and discouraged for very long. They know that if they did, they would eventually lose their passion and start making decisions based on how they are feeling in that moment instead of what they know is best in the long run—for themselves, their students, and their colleagues.

Lao Tzu suggested that, "The journey of a thousand miles begins with a single step." Wherever you are on your journey as an excellent educator, we encourage you to *start right now* to become even greater still—our kids are worth it. This book is not meant to be a step-by-step road map to teaching or leadership excellence, but an overall framework for achieving and sustaining excellence over time. We wish to acknowledge and thank educators everywhere for making a commitment to excellence and staying the course, even when the journey is arduous and requires great personal sacrifice. Thank you for seeing possibilities where others see only problems. Our future is in your hands—and we feel pretty good about that.

REFERENCES

CHAPTER 1

1. "Teacher Leader Model Standards." Accessed November 11, 2016, http://www.teacherleaderstandards.org.

2. York-Barr, Jennifer, and Karen Duke. "What Do We Know About Teacher Leadership? Findings from Two Decades of Scholarship." *Review of Educational Research,* 74, no. 3 (Fall 2004): 255-316.

3. Harrison, Cindy, and Joellen Killion. "Ten Roles for Teacher Leaders." *Educational Leadership,* 65, no. 1 (September 2007): 74-77.

4. Robinson, Viviane. *Student-Centered Leadership: Jossey-Bass Leadership Library in Education.* San Francisco: Jossey-Bass, 2011.

CHAPTER 2

1. Saphier, Jon, Mary Ann Haley-Speca, and Robert Gower. *The Skillful Teacher: Building Your Teaching Skills.* 6th ed. Research for Better Teaching, Inc., 2008.

2. ibid.

3. Collins, Jim. *Good to Great: Why Some Companies Make the Leap...and Others Don't.* New York: Harper Collins, 2001.

4. Covey, Stephen. *The 7 Habits of Highly Effective People: Powerful Lessons in Personal Change.* New York: Simon & Schuster, 1989, 137.

5. Vozza, Stephanie. "Personal Mission Statements of 5 Famous CEOs (And Why You Should Write One Too.)" *Fast Company*

Leadership, February 25, 2014. https://www.fastcompany.com/
3026791/dialed/personal-mission-statements-of-5-famous-ceos-
and-why-you-should-write-one-too.

6. Gonzalez, Jennifer. "A 4-Part System for Getting to Know Your
    Students. *Cult of Pedagogy* (blog), July 10, 2016. http://www.
    cultofpedagogy.com/relationship-building/.

7. Sinek, Simon. "How Great Leaders Inspire Action." TED Talk,
    18:04. Filmed September 2009. https://www.ted.com/talks/
    simon_sinek_how_great_leaders_inspire_action?language=en.

8. "How to Write a Mission Statement That Doesn't Suck." YouTube
    video, 3:51. Posted by *Fast Company*, September 16, 2010. https://
    www.youtube.com/watch?v=LJhG3HZ7b4o.

CHAPTER 3

1. Whitaker, Todd. *What Great Teachers Do Differently: 17 Things
    That Matter Most.* 2nd ed. New York: Routledge, 2012, 103.

2. Couros, George. *The Innovator's Mindset: Empower Learning,
    Unleash Talent, and Lead a Culture of Creativity.* San Diego: Dave
    Burgess Consulting, Inc., 2015.

3. Naisbitt, John, Nana Naisbitt, and Doug Philips. *High Tech High
    Touch: Technology and Our Accelerated Search for Meaning.*
    London: Nicholas Brealey Limited, 2001.

4. Duncan, Roger Dean. "In Times of Change, 'What's in It for
    Me?' Is the Question You Need to Answer," *Fast Company*,
    September 14, 2012. https://www.fastcompany.com/3001250/
    times-change-whats-it-me-question-you-need-answer.

5. Pink, Daniel H. *Drive: The Surprising Truth About What
    Motivates Us.* New York: Riverhead Books, 2011.

6. Heath, Chip and Dan Heath. *Made to Stick: Why Some Ideas
    Survive and Others Die.* New York: Random House, 2008.

7. Friedman, Thomas L. *The World Is Flat: A Brief History of the Twenty-first Century - Updated and Expanded.* New York: Farrar, Straus and Giroux, 2006, 314.

8. "How to Write an Inspiring Vision Statement." YouTube video, 4:33. Posted by "RapidStart Leadership," January 6, 2016. https://www.youtube.com/watch?v=bkTXc2oDWNQ.

9. Heath, Chip and Dan Heath. "Teaching That Sticks." Heath Brothers. 2010. Accessed November 11, 2016. http://heathbrothers.com/download/mts-teaching-that-sticks.pdf.

10. DuFour, Richard, Rebecca DuFour, Robert Eaker, Thomas W. Many, and Mike Mattos. *Learning by Doing: A Handbook for Professional Learning Communities at Work*™. Bloomington, IN: Solution Tree Press, 2016.

11. "30 Example Vision Statements." *Top Nonprofits,* https://topnonprofits.com/examples/vision-statements/.

12. "Daniel Pink—Autonomy, Mastery & Purpose." YouTube video, 5:11. Posted by "sonabasu," January 4, 2012. https://www.youtube.com/watch?v=wdzHgN7_Hs8.

CHAPTER 4

1. "A Lesson in Customer Service from Chick-fil-A President Dan Cathy." S.A.S. N.d. Accessed November 11, 2016. http://www.sas.com/en_us/insights/articles/marketing/a-lesson-in-customer-service-from-chick-fil-a.html/.

2. "Mark Scharenbroich *Official* Nice Bike preview." YouTube video, 12:43. Posted by "Mark Scharenbroich," May 5, 2015. https://www.youtube.com/watch?v=itueLVzd1_M.

3. DeWitt, Peter. "What Are the Best Strategies for Surface to Deep Learning?" *Education Week* (blog), August 21, 2016. http://blogs.edweek.org/edweek/

finding_common_ground/2016/08/what_are_the_best_
strategies_for%20surface_to_deep_learning.html.

CHAPTER 5

1. Dweck, Carol. *Mindset: The New Psychology of Success.* New York: Ballatine Books, 2007.

2. Hemingway, Ernest. *The Sun Also Rises.* New York: Scribner, 1954.

3. Bronson, Po. "How Not to Talk to Your Kids: The inverse power of praise." *New York Magazine*, August 3, 2007. http://nymag.com/news/features/27840/.

4. Whitaker, Todd, Jeffery Zoul, and Jimmy Casas. *What Connected Educators Do Differently.* New York: Routledge, 2015.

5. Hattie, John. *Visible Learning: A Synthesis of Over 800 Meta-Analyses Relating to Achievement.* New York: Routledge, 2009.

6. Durant, Will. *The Story of Philosophy: The Lives and Opinions of the World's Greatest Philosophers* (1926). Simon & Schuster/Pocket Books, 1991.

7. Kuriyama, Cesar. "One Second Every Day" TED Talk, 8:02. Filmed March 2012. http://www.ted.com/talks/cesar_kuriyama_one_second_every_day?language=en.

CHAPTER 6

1. Wikipedia contributors. "Excellence." Wikipedia, The Free Encyclopedia, November 8, 2016. https://en.wikipedia.org/w/index.php?title=Excellence&oldid=748570386.

Teach Like a PIRATE

Increase Student Engagement, Boost Your Creativity, and Transform Your Life as an Educator

By Dave Burgess (@BurgessDave)

Teach Like a PIRATE is the *New York Times'* best-selling book that has sparked a worldwide educational revolution. It is part inspirational manifesto that ignites passion for the profession, and part practical road map filled with dynamic strategies to dramatically increase student engagement. Translated into multiple languages, its message resonates with educators who want to design outrageously creative lessons and transform school into a life-changing experience for students.

P is for PIRATE

Inspirational ABC's for Educators

By Dave and Shelley Burgess (@Burgess_Shelley)

Teaching is an adventure that stretches the imagination and calls for creativity every day! In *P is for Pirate*, husband and wife team, Dave and Shelley Burgess, encourage and inspire educators to make their classrooms fun and exciting places to learn. Tapping into years of personal experience and drawing on the insights of more than seventy educators, the authors offer a wealth of ideas for making learning and teaching more fulfilling than ever before.

The Innovator's Mindset

Empower Learning, Unleash Talent, and Lead a
Culture of Creativity
By George Couros (@gcouros)

The traditional system of education requires students to hold their questions and compliantly stick to the scheduled curriculum. But our job as educators is to provide new and better opportunities for our students. It's time to recognize that compliance doesn't foster innovation, encourage critical thinking, or inspire creativity—and those are the skills our students need to succeed. In *The Innovator's Mindset*, George Couros encourages teachers and administrators to empower their learners to wonder, to explore—and to become forward-thinking leaders.

Pure Genius

Building a Culture of Innovation and Taking
20% Time to the Next Level
By Don Wettrick (@DonWettrick)

For far too long, schools have been bastions of boredom, killers of creativity, and way too comfortable with compliance and conformity. In *Pure Genius*, Don Wettrick explains how collaboration—with experts, students, and other educators—can help you create interesting, and even life-changing, opportunities for learning. Wettrick's book inspires and equips educators with a systematic blueprint for teaching innovation in any school.

Learn Like a PIRATE
Empower Your Students to Collaborate, Lead, and Succeed

By Paul Solarz (@PaulSolarz)

Today's job market demands that students be prepared to take responsibility for their lives and careers. We do them a disservice if we teach them how to earn passing grades without equipping them to take charge of their education. In *Learn Like a PIRATE*, Paul Solarz explains how to design classroom experiences that encourage students to take risks and explore their passions in a stimulating, motivating, and supportive environment where improvement, rather than grades, is the focus. Discover how student-led classrooms help students thrive and develop into self-directed, confident citizens who are capable of making smart, responsible decisions, all on their own.

Ditch That Textbook
Free Your Teaching and Revolutionize Your Classroom

By Matt Miller (@jmattmiller)

Textbooks are symbols of centuries-old education. They're often outdated as soon as they hit students' desks. Acting "by the textbook" implies compliance and a lack of creativity. It's time to ditch those textbooks—and those textbook assumptions about learning! In *Ditch That Textbook*, teacher and blogger Matt Miller encourages educators to throw out meaningless, pedestrian teaching and learning practices. He empowers them to evolve and improve on old, standard teaching methods. *Ditch That Textbook* is a support system, toolbox, and manifesto to help educators free their teaching and revolutionize their classrooms.

50 Things You Can Do with Google Classroom

By Alice Keeler and Libbi Miller (@alicekeeler, @MillerLibbi)

It can be challenging to add new technology to the classroom but it's a must if students are going to be well-equipped for the future. Alice Keeler and Libbi Miller shorten the learning curve by providing a thorough overview of the Google Classroom App. Part of Google Apps for Education (GAfE), Google Classroom was specifically designed to help teachers save time by streamlining the process of going digital. Complete with screenshots, *50 Things You Can Do with Google Classroom* provides ideas and step-by-step instructions to help teachers implement this powerful tool.

50 Things to Go Further with Google Classroom

A Student-Centered Approach

By Alice Keeler and Libbi Miller (@alicekeeler, @MillerLibbi)

Today's technology empowers educators to move away from the traditional classroom where teachers lead and students work independently—each doing the same thing. In *50 Things to Go Further with Google Classroom: A Student-Centered Approach*, authors and educators Alice Keeler and Libbi Miller offer inspiration and resources to help you create a digitally rich, engaging, student-centered environment. They show you how to tap into the power of individualized learning that is possible with Google Classroom.

140 Twitter Tips for Educators

Get Connected, Grow Your Professional Learning Network, and Reinvigorate Your Career

By Brad Currie, Billy Krakower, and Scott Rocco (@bradmcurrie, @wkrakower, @ScottRRocco)

Whatever questions you have about education or about how you can be even better at your job, you'll find ideas, resources, and a vibrant network of professionals ready to help you on Twitter. In *140 Twitter Tips for Educators*, #Satchat hosts and founders of Evolving Educators, Brad Currie, Billy Krakower, and Scott Rocco offer step-by-step instructions to help you master the basics of Twitter, build an online following, and become a Twitter rock star.

Master the Media

How Teaching Media Literacy Can Save Our Plugged-in World

By Julie Smith (@julnilsmith)

Written to help teachers and parents educate the next generation, *Master the Media* explains the history, purpose, and messages behind the media. The point isn't to get kids to unplug; it's to help them make informed choices, understand the difference between truth and lies, and discern perception from reality. Critical thinking leads to smarter decisions— and it's why media literacy can save the world.

The Zen Teacher

Creating Focus, Simplicity, and Tranquility in the Classroom

By Dan Tricarico (@thezenteacher)

Teachers have incredible power to influence—even improve—the future. In *The Zen Teacher,* educator, blogger, and speaker Dan Tricarico provides practical, easy-to-use techniques to help teachers be their best—unrushed and fully focused—so they can maximize their performance and improve their quality of life. In this introductory guide, Dan Tricarico explains what it means to develop a Zen practice—something that has nothing to do with religion and everything to do with your ability to thrive in the classroom.

eXPlore Like a Pirate

Gamification and Game-Inspired Course Design to Engage, Enrich, and Elevate Your Learners

By Michael Matera (@MrMatera)

Are you ready to transform your classroom into an experiential world that flourishes on collaboration and creativity? Then set sail with classroom game designer and educator Michael Matera as he reveals the possibilities and power of game-based learning. In *eXPlore Like a Pirate*, Matera serves as your experienced guide to help you apply the most motivational techniques of gameplay to your classroom. You'll learn gamification strategies that will work with and enhance (rather than replace) your current curriculum and discover how these engaging methods can be applied to any grade level or subject.

Your School Rocks ... So Tell People!
Passionately Pitch and Promote the Positives
Happening on Your Campus
By Ryan McLane and Eric Lowe (@McLane_Ryan,
@EricLowe21)

Great things are happening in your school every day. The problem is, no one beyond your school walls knows about them. School principals Ryan McLane and Eric Lowe want to help you get the word out! In *Your School Rocks... So Tell People!* McLane and Lowe offer more than seventy immediately actionable tips along with easy-to-follow instructions and links to video tutorials. This practical guide will equip you to create an effective and manageable communication strategy using social media tools. Learn how to keep your students' families and community connected, informed, and excited about what's going on in your school.

Play Like a Pirate
Engage Students with Toys, Games, and Comics
By Quinn Rollins (@jedikermit)

Yes! Serious learning can be seriously fun. In *Play Like a Pirate*, Quinn Rollins offers practical, engaging strategies and resources that make it easy to integrate fun into your curriculum. Regardless of the grade level you teach, you'll find inspiration and ideas that will help you engage your students in unforgettable ways.

The Classroom Chef

Sharpen your lessons. Season your classes. Make math meaningful.

By John Stevens and Matt Vaudrey
(@Jstevens009, @MrVaudrey)

In *The Classroom Chef*, math teachers and instructional coaches John Stevens and Matt Vaudrey share their secret recipes, ingredients, and tips for serving up lessons that engage students and help them "get" math. You can use these ideas and methods as-is, or better yet, tweak them and create your own enticing educational meals. The message the authors share is that, with imagination and preparation, every teacher can be a Classroom Chef.

How Much Water Do We Have?

5 Success Principles for Conquering Any Challenge and Thriving in Times of Change
By Pete Nunweiler with Kris Nunweiler

In *How Much Water Do We Have?* Pete Nunweiler identifies five key elements—information, planning, motivation, support, and leadership—that are necessary for the success of any goal, life transition, or challenge. Referring to these elements as the 5 Waters of Success, Pete explains that like the water we drink, you need them to thrive in today's rapidly paced world. If you're feeling stressed out, overwhelmed, or uncertain at work or at home, pause and look for the signs of dehydration. Learn how to find, acquire, and use the 5 Waters of Success—so you can share them with your team and family members.

The Writing on the Classroom Wall
How Posting Your Most Passionate Beliefs about
Education Can Empower Your Students, Propel
Your Growth, and Lead to a Lifetime of Learning
By Steve Wyborney (@SteveWyborney)

In *The Writing on the Classroom Wall*, Steve Wyborney explains how posting and discussing Big Ideas can lead to deeper learning. You'll learn why sharing your ideas will sharpen and refine them. You'll also be encouraged to know that the Big Ideas you share don't have to be profound to make a profound impact on learning. In fact, Steve explains, it's okay if some of your ideas fall off the wall. What matters most is sharing them.

Kids Deserve It!
Pushing Boundaries and Challenging
Conventional Thinking
By Todd Nesloney and Adam Welcome
(@TechNinjaTodd, @awelcome)

In *Kids Deserve It!*, Todd and Adam encourage you to think big and make learning fun and meaningful for students. Their high-tech, high-touch, and highly engaging practices will inspire you to take risks, shake up the status quo, and be a champion for your students. While you're at it, you just might rediscover why you became an educator in the first place.

LAUNCH

Using Design Thinking to Boost Creativity and Bring Out the Maker in Every Student

By John Spencer and A.J. Juliani

(@spencerideas, @ajjuliani)

Something happens in students when they define themselves as makers and inventors and creators. They discover powerful skills—problem-solving, critical thinking, and imagination—that will help them shape the world's future...our future. In *LAUNCH*, John Spencer and A.J. Juliani provide a process that can be incorporated into every class at every grade level...even if you don't consider yourself a "creative teacher." And if you dare to innovate and view creativity as an essential skill, you will empower your students to change the world—starting right now.

Instant Relevance

Using Today's Experiences in Tomorrow's Lessons

By Denis Sheeran (@MathDenisNJ)

Every day, students in schools around the world ask the question, "When am I ever going to use this in real life?" In *Instant Relevance*, author and keynote speaker Denis Sheeran equips you to create engaging lessons from experiences and events that matter to your students. Learn how to help your students see meaningful connections between the real word and what they learn in the classroom—because that's when learning sticks.

Escaping the School Leader's Dunk Tank
*How to Prevail When Others Want to
See You Drown*
Rebecca Coda and Rick Jetter
(@RebeccaCoda, @RickJetter)

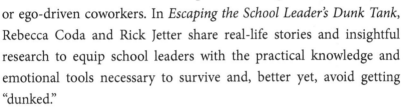

No school leader is immune to the dunk tank—
the effects of discrimination, bad politics, revenge,
or ego-driven coworkers. In *Escaping the School Leader's Dunk Tank*,
Rebecca Coda and Rick Jetter share real-life stories and insightful
research to equip school leaders with the practical knowledge and
emotional tools necessary to survive and, better yet, avoid getting
"dunked."

ABOUT THE AUTHORS

Todd Whitaker, PhD, has been fortunate to be able to blend his passion with his career. Recognized as a leading presenter in the field of education, his message about the importance of teaching has resonated with hundreds of thousands of educators around the world. Todd is a professor of educational leadership at the University of Missouri, and he has spent his life pursuing his love of education by researching and studying effective teachers and principals.

Prior to moving into higher education, he was a math teacher and basketball coach in Missouri. Todd then served as a principal at the middle-school, junior-high, and high-school levels. He was also a middle-school coordinator in charge of staffing, curriculum, and technology for the opening of new middle schools.

One of the nation's leading authorities on staff motivation, teacher leadership, and principal effectiveness, Todd has written more than thirty books, including the national bestseller *What Great Teachers Do Differently*. Other titles include: *Shifting the Monkey, Dealing with Difficult Teachers, The Ten-Minute Inservice, The Ball, What Great Principals Do Differently, Motivating & Inspiring Teachers*, and a previous collaboration with Jimmy and Jeff, *What Connected Educators Do Differently*. Please follow and contact Todd via Twitter: @ToddWhitaker.

Jeffrey Zoul, EdD, is a lifelong teacher, learner, and leader, currently serving as Assistant Superintendent for Teaching and Learning with Deerfield Public Schools District 109 in Deerfield, Illinois. Prior to working in this capacity, Jeff served as a district administrator in Rock Island, Illinois, and a school improvement specialist with Southern Regional Education Board (SREB), the nation's largest and oldest non-profit school improvement network. Jeff also served as a principal with Forsyth County Schools in Cumming, Georgia, and with North Shore School District 112 in Highland Park, Illinois.

Before serving as an administrator, Zoul was a classroom teacher for eighteen years in Georgia, teaching elementary school, middle school, and high-school English.

Jeff is also the author of several books, including *Improving Your School One Week at a Time: Building the Foundation for Professional Teaching and Learning, 4 CORE Factors for School Success* (co-authored with Todd Whitaker), and *What Connected Educators Do Differently* (a collaboration with Todd Whitaker and Jimmy Casas). Jeff has also served as an adjunct professor at University of North Georgia, teaching graduate-level courses in research and assessment. In 2014, he was awarded the Bammy Educators Voice Award.

Jeff earned a bachelor of arts degree in education from the University of Massachusetts at Amherst and a master of science degree in education from Troy University. In addition, Zoul earned an education specialist's degree from the University of Southern Mississippi and a doctoral degree from the University of Alabama in Tuscaloosa, Alabama. Please follow and contact Jeff via Twitter: @Jeff_Zoul.

Jimmy Casas recently completed his twenty-second year in educational leadership. He received his bachelor of arts in Spanish and masters in teaching from the University of Iowa and his masters in administrative leadership from Cardinal Stritch University in Milwaukee. Jimmy is currently working on his Ed.S. at Drake University in Des Moines and also serves as an adjunct professor for Drake, teaching a graduate course on educational leadership. His passion for teaching and learning, coupled with a vision for developing a community of leaders, has procured a culture of excellence and high standards for learning amid a positive school culture for students and staff. Under his leadership, Bettendorf High School was named one of the Best High Schools in the country three times by Newsweek and US News & World Report. Jimmy's core purpose lies in serving others.

Jimmy was named the 2012 Iowa Secondary Principal of the Year, and was selected as one of three finalists for NASSP 2013 National Secondary Principal of the Year. In 2013, he received the Bammy Educators Voice Award as the Secondary School Principal of the Year. In 2014, Jimmy was invited to the White House to speak on the Future Ready Schools pledge. In 2015, Jimmy received the Bammy Award for National Secondary Principal of the Year. He is the co-founder of EdCampIowa and also the co-founder of #IAedchat, an online chat that takes place every Sunday evening at 8:00 p.m. CST. Finally, Jimmy is the coauthor, in a previous collaboration with Todd and Jeff, of *What Connected Educators Do Differently*. Please follow and contact Jimmy via Twitter: @casas_jimmy.

Made in the USA
Lexington, KY
13 March 2017